THE PRINCIPLES OF FRANCHISEE SUCCESS

APPLY THEM

AND TAKE CONTROL OF YOUR BUSINESS RESULTS

Written by

Laura Darrell, MA Leadership

Copyright © 2023 Laura Darrell

All rights reserved.

INTRODUCTION

In my first book, *The Great Resignation*, I highlighted the need for business leaders to focus on their organizational health, specifically how appreciative and coaching leadership could help build a company culture that puts employees first and ultimately yields better business results. Knowing that working for an organization like this isn't the reality for many working people today, I wrote a follow-up book, *The Promotability Gap*. This book highlighted the top reasons people fail to advance in their careers and specific development initiatives that, in the absence of managers who support employees with their professional development, could help them develop on their own and achieve greater career success.

My new book, *The Principles of Franchisee Success*, is for those who, for various reasons, have decided to leave corporate life behind to pursue the dream of owning their own business. Becoming an entrepreneur can be a scary proposition for those currently working in the relative security of the corporate world. A business failure rate of over 70% [1] stops many from taking the leap because they deem the risk too significant. What if I fail? What if I can't replace my salary with profit from my business? How will I take care of my family? Pay my mortgage? The list of concerns gets longer and longer with each passing thought. Well, with a franchised business failure rate, at the top one hundred franchises in North America as low as 2 % [2] and a completely re-imagined world of work where people are leaving corporate America in droves [3], it's not surprising that many people are overcoming their fear of small business failure by joining the ever-increasing number of franchisees in North America.

The USA, with over 750,000 franchised business units, and Canada, with over 75,000 franchised business units, hold the top two spots globally for the overall number of franchises. Every day ordinary people from many different backgrounds choose to take a safer approach to entrepreneurship and buy into a franchise system. While this is a terrific option for those a little less risk-averse to ultimately going out on their own, there is much to learn and understand about the franchisee/franchisor working relationship before jumping into one of the many franchised opportunities across almost every industry today.

Illuminating the Problem

Having spent over two decades working in the franchised world, I've seen the relationship between franchisees and franchisors operate from both sides of the fence. Early in my career, I 'grew up,' so to speak, in the world of franchisees. Working for over ten years at A&W Restaurants, a leading Canadian quick service restaurant franchise [4], for five different multi-unit franchisees, I saw firsthand good and bad examples of how franchisees operated their businesses. I observed how they built and maintained a relationship with the franchisor, became financially successful, and continued expanding their portfolio of locations.

Adding to my franchise experience, I spent another ten years working for two of the most successful Canadian full-service restaurant franchisors, White Spot Restaurants [5] and Boston Pizza Restaurants [6]. I held increasingly senior leadership roles, starting as a Regional Manager at Triple O's by White Spot and ending my career as Vice President of Operations and Training at Boston Pizza. While working in operations roles with these two franchisors, I built relationships with hundreds of franchisees across Canada. I saw firsthand how franchisees who consistently focused their efforts on three fundamental principles, building collaborative relationships, consistent execution, and a commitment to their communities, delivered incredible results. Alternatively, I experienced many franchisees who ran their business below operating standards, ignored the relationships in their community, and built disagreeable relationships with their franchisor and other key stakeholders. I'm sure you can guess what kind of business results they achieved.

What Will You Learn?

The Principles of Franchisee Success takes the best of my knowledge from both my franchisee and franchisor experiences. You'll learn how the typical profile of a franchisee differs from those who work corporately for the franchisor. You'll understand which two departments at the franchisor's head office have the most significant impact on the franchisee and their success and how they should work together to enhance franchisee business results. You'll get a behind-the-scenes look at how successful franchisors train and develop their teams to understand the business from the franchisees' perspective and communication strategies that ensure both the franchisee and franchisor are on the same page. We'll also take a deep dive into operating a successful franchised unit, regardless of its industry, and how a focus on consistent execution of the brand standards, specifically the customer experience, can drive better business results and enhance your relationship with the franchisor. We'll explore what questions you should ask your franchisor or potential franchisors about the health of their system, their working relationships with their franchisees, and what they deem to be the most important characteristics of those achieving solid results within their brand. Finally, we'll explore franchisees' relationships with their communities and why those relationships matter to your success and the brand's success. Franchisees and franchisors are cut from two different cloths. Understanding each stakeholder's perspective, work style and drivers of success in this dynamic relationship can lead to enhanced success and business results for all.

Where Did These Strategies Come From?

The strategies put forward in this book come from over two decades of experience working for successful franchisees and leading franchisors in Canada. They have been designed, evaluated, and enhanced in the field with franchisees and operations professionals from business units of differing sales volume and size in both rural and urban locations. My practical hands-on experience working with franchisees and franchisors has been enhanced by my formal education, a master's degree in leadership from Royal Roads University. During this intense program, my research focused on how collaborative relationships between franchisees and franchisors could lead to enhanced business outcomes for both key stakeholders.

I undertook a capstone project that had me use a multi-method research approach to understand from both perspectives what success looks like in the critical areas of franchisor support from the operations and marketing departments and how meaningful communication and points of engagement with franchisees lead to a more collaborative and positive working relationship. During this research approach, I learned of many examples of successful collaborative initiatives within a franchised system and many examples otherwise. Times when franchisees felt unsupported and like their ideas and concerns went unheard, leading to feelings of frustration and helplessness. I'll share examples of both situations to help shine a light on what right looks like and how you, as a franchisee, can work to role model this collaborative behavior in your engagements with your franchisor.

Turning this Book into Action

I've written this book in three parts, each focusing on a core principle of franchisee success: collaboration, community, and consistency that, when simultaneously put into action, will help you achieve strong unit economics that will enhance your profitability and ability to grow your business further. Each chapter in these sections wraps up with reflective questions that can help you understand how these principles are operating within your existing franchise or how to use these reflective questions when determining which franchise you'll invest in, both with your time and money.

Working within a franchised system has many significant benefits when starting your entrepreneurial journey. You have a strong safety net that includes tried and tested operating systems, tools, and standards. You benefit from a collective marketing effort that works to build the brand and your business. And you have access to a system of franchisees with many best practices to share to help you mitigate problems they may have experienced early on in their journey. However, as I've suggested already, if you want to get the most out of this often-complex relationship, there needs to be a balance between what benefits the franchisor and what benefits the franchisee. With this book, I aim to help existing, and potential franchisees build strong and mutually beneficial relationships with those who work for the franchisor, enhancing unit economics for the franchisee and system economics for the franchisor. Let's dive in!

CONTENTS

INTRODUCTION i

PRINCIPLE ONE: A Collaborative Relationship with Your Franchisor is Essential to Your Success 1

CHAPTER ONE 3
    Understanding the Franchisee-Franchisor Relationship
CHAPTER ONE REFLECTIVE QUESTIONS 12

CHAPTER TWO 15
    Trust is the Foundation of Collaborative Relationships
CHAPTER TWO REFLECTIVE QUESTIONS 24

CHAPTER THREE 27
    Communication is the Cornerstone of Collaborative Success
CHAPTER THREE REFLECTIVE QUESTIONS 38

CHAPTER FOUR 41
    How Marketing and Operations Impact Franchised Business Results
CHAPTER FOUR REFLECTIVE QUESTIONS 51

PRINCIPLE TWO: Consistency is What Makes a Franchised System Successful 53

CHAPTER FIVE 55
    Consistent Execution of Brand Standards is Required for Franchisee Success
CHAPTER FIVE REFLECTIVE QUESTIONS 63

CHAPTER SIX 65
    Consistently Executed Training Leads to Consistent Operations

CHAPTER SIX REFLECTIVE QUESTIONS 72

CHAPTER SEVEN 75
    How Franchisors Manage 'Best Practices' is Critical to Consistent Execution

CHAPTER SEVEN REFLECTIVE QUESTIONS 83

CHAPTER EIGHT 85
    Consistent Local Marketing Efforts Enhance Unit Economics

CHAPTER EIGHT REFLECTIVE QUESTIONS 92

PRINCIPLE THREE: Community Connections Help Your Business Thrive 95

CHAPTER NINE 97
    Why Community Relationships Matter

CHAPTER NINE REFLECTIVE QUESTIONS 103

CHAPTER TEN 105
    Building Community Relationships That Last

CHAPTER TEN REFLECTIVE QUESTIONS 112

CHAPTER ELEVEN 115
    Strengthening Your Online Community

CHAPTER ELEVEN REFLECTIVE QUESTIONS 121

PUTTING IT ALL TOGETHER 123

SOURCES 127

PRINCIPLE ONE

A Collaborative Relationship with Your Franchisor is Essential to Your Success

CHAPTER ONE

Understanding the Franchisee-Franchisor Relationship

The relationship between franchisees and their franchisor can be complex and challenging. Both stakeholders have differences that, when not viewed and understood from an appreciative stance, can lead to a difficult path filled with friction and frustration by both groups. It's vital to understand that as a franchisee, there are many relationships to manage with your franchisor. Your overall relationship will consist of several individual relationships with employees who work for the franchisor. It's an important distinction to understand because employees within an organization think and act very differently than entrepreneurial franchisees running their businesses.

The franchisor is often structured as a functional

organization divided into departments focused on specialized business areas, such as marketing, operations, information technology, design and construction, and human resources. While these departments provide the opportunity to create greater operational efficiencies between individuals with similar skill sets working closely together, they can also cause challenges for franchisees within the system, particularly with communication and collaboration. It can be challenging for franchisees to understand who works in each department and what precisely they do to support the franchised business units.

The franchisees' business unit operates in a much more streamlined fashion, with usually a General Manager if the franchisee isn't filling this position themselves and a small team of employees to service the customers' needs. Everything happens much quicker at the franchisee level; the team identifies problems and raises them to management, who then addresses or escalates them to the franchisor, sometimes within hours. Dealing with a franchisor with multiple departments and management layers built into their hierarchy means that communication and solutions will take more time, which can be very frustrating when you are working on the frontlines of the business.

Another key difference that impacts the relationship between franchisees and their franchisors is the fundamental characteristic differences between people who pursue entrepreneurship and those who seek a corporate career. Entrepreneurs have several key personality traits that often contrast the types of individuals who pursue careers within a typical organization, specifically *curiosity, risk tolerance*, and *adaptability* [7]. Let's look at these traits in contrast to those of employees working within a franchisor's organization.

Curiosity

Successful franchisee entrepreneurs often have an increased level of curiosity, and it's that ability to remain curious that leads them to continuously ask questions about why specific promotions were chosen over others or why operating standards were designed the way they were. They have an intrinsic desire to explore different solutions and ideas. When they aren't included in the exploration or ideation phases of new programs, systems, or tools, this cuts directly against their curious nature.

Alternatively, when you look at the average employee working within an organization, you'll see that while they often have the desire to be more curious, exploring new ideas and ways of doing things, they often work for senior leaders in their departments who prefer consistency and efficiency over curious exploration. A study by Francesca Gino, a professor at Harvard Business School, found that over 70% of employees faced daily barriers to being inquisitive and asking more questions while on the job [8]. She concluded her research by suggesting that, in most organizations, managers and employees receive the unspoken message that asking questions is an inferred challenge to the organization's executive authority. The managers and employees within organizations are often trained to focus solely on their day-to-day duties without paying much attention to the process or the organization's overall goals, leading to a significant decline in creativity and innovation [9].

Nurturing a spirit of curiosity within the franchisor's head office could yield significant benefits. First, to the financial results of the business, both for the franchisor and the franchisee and second, to an enhanced collaborative relationship with franchisees whose curious nature often leads them to innovative ways of solving problems.

Risk Taking

Starting your own business can be a risky proposition. Research conducted by the US Bureau of Labor Statistics found that over 70% of small businesses ultimately fail; sadly, these are pre-COVID-19 numbers [10]. In light of this sobering statistic, would-be entrepreneurs know that they must prepare themselves and be comfortable with the chance that their business may fail; this is one of the reasons buying a franchise is so appealing to new entrepreneurs. In exchange for paying a 'franchise fee', they buy into a proven business model with ample support. That support often materializes through well-established operational systems and tools and a robust marketing program to help them drive unit sales. So, rather than letting the fear of failure hold them back, savvy entrepreneurs instead focus on the possibility of success and let that propel them forward.

Employees of the franchisor's organization often have a different mindset regarding risk and failure, and it's not entirely their fault. In traditional organizational structures, employees are rewarded for their successful work in three ways: appreciation for a job well done, a merit increase during their annual performance review, and promotion into more senior positions. This is how the typical corporate career is built. Failure is often considered a failed attempt to fulfill their work duties satisfactorily, which drives employee behavior not associated with taking additional risks. In most organizations, both franchisor and otherwise, you'll find employees who do the job strictly as they've been trained to do it or how it has historically been performed. Taking risks to think outside the box and do things differently could lead to poor manager reviews, negative monetary consequences, a stalled career, or, worse yet, losing your job. All of these fears are real at the employee level.

Franchisors would be well served to create an environment that encourages innovative thinking and a certain level of risk-taking at the employee and manager levels to help drive business results and innovation while enhancing the relatability between their franchisees and those who work to support them. Taking a page from some of the tech companies could be beneficial here. Google, for example, allows employees to spend 20% of their time solely innovating and working on new ideas or skills [11]. 3M, another organization reliant on constant innovation, allows 15% of employees' time to be spent dreaming up the next big idea [12]. An approach like this implemented at the franchisor's head office could lead to valuable collaboration between key stakeholders, a way to plug into the creative instincts of the systems' entrepreneurial franchisees.

Adaptability

The need for strong skills in adaptability to change has never been so obvious. COVID-19 and its devastating impact on entrepreneurs and small businesses throughout the western world pushed this vital characteristic to the top of the must-have list, and with good reason. The response to the pandemic was fluid and changed frequently based on direction from the government and local health authorities. I witnessed this firsthand as Vice President of Operations and Training at Boston Pizza, one of Canada's most admired franchised restaurant chains. Franchisees who were able to continually re-evaluate the changing business environment and adapt to the current situation kept moving their business forward, regardless of what was happening around them. They had a laser focus on business continuance, and if that meant adapting, seemingly daily, to changes in well-established operating procedures, they dug in and made it happen. In comparison, those who panicked and failed to adjust to the new working environment suffered further business losses.

It's widely accepted that we live in a time of constant change, making adaptability an in-demand skill set for entrepreneurs and employees alike. Having employees who can adapt to times of uncertainty and unwanted change is critical, as is their ability to adapt to changes in the organizations' programs, systems, and tools. Business evolves rapidly, and their ability to adapt is critical, especially when the livelihoods and investment capital of the system's franchisees is on the line. If adaptability to change is such an important skill, why is it so difficult for organizations to adequately execute change initiatives within the system?

One of the main reasons change initiatives fall short at the organizational level is that senior leaders and executives fail to understand the various stages of personal transformation. This frequently leads to the need for an adequate change plan to be deployed alongside the change initiatives. John Kotter, a leading expert on all things change-related [13], suggests that people must move through eight stages of change for the change initiative or behavior to take hold. Franchisors would be well-served to ensure that not only are their executive leaders leveraging a change plan alongside any of their change initiatives but that franchisees, specifically those who may struggle with change, have access to internal or external training opportunities that help them understand the various phases of change and where they are getting 'stuck' in the process.

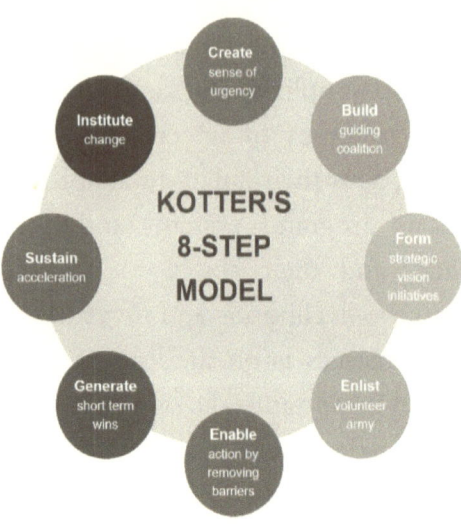

Understanding the critical differences between those who pursue entrepreneurship and those who choose a conventional career within traditional organizations is the key to successful collaboration [14]. The franchisee and the franchisor need each other to succeed; they, in fact, have many shared goals. Franchisors need to attract entrepreneurs into their system, as selling more units is one of the keys to growth. Franchisees also need responsible system growth; the more locations, the more visible the brand is, building consumer awareness for the entire system. The franchisee needs the franchisor to have a strong team of professionals who can design and maintain the programs, systems, and tools required to operate the business model and to ensure that the same business model evolves to meet the changing needs of its customers.

One of the main reasons entrepreneurs select one franchise over another is because of the well-established systems and tools that exist to support the franchisee. So, the franchisors' investment in a highly skilled workforce will not only help to support strong execution in existing business units, but it will also help them to attract more franchisees to the system. One aspect of the business can only succeed with the others.

CHAPTER ONE

REFLECTIVE QUESTIONS

1. How is the franchisors' organization structured? What departments exist to support the system's franchisees?

2. How does the franchisor promote innovation and responsible risk-taking amongst its employees?

3. Does the franchisor have a solid understanding of change management principles? Do they utilize a formal change management plan when undergoing significant change initiatives?

4. Does the franchisor provide franchisees with any change management training resources?

NOTES & REFLECTIONS

CHAPTER TWO

Trust is the Foundation of Collaborative Relationships

Trust is essential in building any collaborative relationship, even more so in a franchised environment. When potential franchisees decide to enter into an agreement with a franchisor, they trust their investment will be well protected and supported. Likewise, when franchisors approve new franchisees into the system, they trust that the franchisee will adhere to all the operational brand standards, ensuring customers have a consistent experience wherever they visit the brand. Understanding the interdependent nature of the importance of trust within the franchise system is critical. *Transparency, consistency*, and *trusted expertise* are the most important aspects of trust in a franchisee-franchisor relationship; let's take a closer look at all three elements.

Transparency

Transparency is often at the top of the list of characteristics needed to build trust in franchisee-franchisor relationships, and for good reason. If I were to give one piece of advice to those reading this book contemplating buying a franchised business, doing your due diligence to understand how transparent the franchisor is, specifically in three key areas, is essential to your decision-making process. Those three areas are how the marketing fund is managed, how supplier rebates are used, and how franchisees who don't follow the brand standards are addressed. Let's look at each of these three areas.

It's very common in the franchised world for franchisees to pay into a marketing fund on top of the franchise fee paid on each dollar their unit earns. The marketing contribution can range from 1% to 4.5%, depending on the brand, making this not an insignificant impact on your overall unit economics. It's important to understand that the monies collected for the marketing or advertising fund are the franchisee's money and are to be spent on building brand awareness and driving traffic to the individual business units. As such, there should be complete transparency in how this money is spent. It would be best to understand how much money collected from franchisees is spent on administrative costs and what those costs are. It would help if you also understood how the fund is divided amongst the markets where the brand operates. A good franchisor partner will fully summarize how these funds are spent annually. If they don't, it should be a red flag around the level of transparency the franchisor is willing to share about the funds they collect to promote and advertise the brand.

Another common transparency issue in a franchised environment comes into play when discussing any supplier rebates the franchisor receives because of the purchasing they do on behalf of the system. Supplier rebates are very common in the restaurant franchise world, and they can be a significant pinch point in the relationship and a roadblock to trust [15]. Trust is eroded if the franchisor isn't transparent about whether these funds go back into the franchisor's profit center or are used for activities that benefit the entire system. In researching this book, I had the opportunity to interview a very successful founder of a US-based franchise, ranked in the top 200 restaurant franchises with hundreds of units and hundreds of millions of dollars in sales. They told me that transparency was so important to them and their relationship with their franchisees that they committed that every supplier rebate given to the franchisor would go back into the building and promoting of the brand and not into the overall profit of the franchisor. This level of transparency is foundational to building trust, so understanding how your franchisor or potential franchisor manages supplier rebates is essential.

The final area where transparency is critical in building a collaborative franchisee-franchisor relationship is how non-compliant franchisees within the system are addressed. The main advantage of buying a franchised business is its significantly lower failure rate. A study by FranNet, one of North America's most respected franchise brokers, found that after five years of business operations, 85% of franchised units were still operating [16]. To protect this low failure rate, all steps must be taken to protect the brand's reputation, built over time on consumers' trust in a consistent customer experience, achieved through franchisee adherence to a well-designed operating system. Franchisees who cut corners, fail to follow the brand standards, or treat their employees poorly risk negative publicity and a poor customer experience that puts the entire system at risk, not to mention the investment dollars of every franchisee. All it takes is one poorly operated unit and a lack of action by the franchisor to put the chain at risk, especially other units within the same local trading area. Ensuring you understand how the franchisor deals with these situations is essential, as other franchisees are largely powerless to correct the issues themselves.

Consistency

Consistency is another core principle of building trust in the franchisee-franchisor relationship, and its importance shows up in several critical areas of the business. The two most meaningful areas of consistency in the franchisee-franchisor relationship, outside of operating the business units, which we discuss in part two of this book, are around how franchisees are treated in the system and how new franchised units are chosen and awarded within the system. Nothing erodes trust more than an inconsistent approach to managing results and system growth.

When entering into a franchised system, it's important to understand how franchisees are treated. I've sometimes experienced big multi-unit franchisees being given more leeway regarding poor operations, as franchisors can be hesitant to use a heavy hand with someone who owns multiple units in the system. Regardless of the franchisee, dealing with underperforming locations is critical irrespective of how many units the franchisee may own. Because as we discussed above, franchise success is built upon consistent execution of the franchise's programs, systems, and tools, and at the end of the day, the customer who has a negative experience doesn't often know, let alone care if the franchisee owns twenty locations or one. A bad experience is a bad experience and poses a significant risk to the brand's success, so trusting that your franchisor will handle all franchisees in the same manner as it relates to underperformance is critical.

The other main area where consistency comes into play when building and maintaining trust in the relationship between franchisees and franchisors has to do with how the system grows. Not only as it relates to how system growth impacts existing franchised locations but also how those growth opportunities are awarded within the system of existing franchisees. A transparent approach to both, executed consistently across the system, is crucial for building trust.

Unit growth is a core tenant of how franchisors measure the success of their brand and when done sustainably, provides benefits to existing franchisees as well. The more locations the brand has, the more brand awareness the system generates amongst consumers, building individual unit sales and sales for the entire system. New unit growth can become a detraction on individual franchisee success when the franchisor undertakes a growth-at-all-cost mentality, in other words, irresponsible growth. Too many units in the same trading area can negatively impact same-unit sales growth year-over-year. While the franchisor will likely continue to grow its top-line sales through increasing units, the individual franchisee could see their sales decline if an additional unit is opened too close to their location.

Ensuring you understand how growth is determined within your franchised system is important to your overall success. How are new locations selected? What tools or processes do they use to assess the viability of that location and its potential cannibalization of sales on existing units? Great franchisors have a scientific approach to making these decisions and will openly share that process with franchisees whom the new location may impact. Also, franchisees must understand how growth opportunities are awarded within the franchised system. All too often, backroom deals with large multi-unit groups are the preferred approach to awarding new locations. While I agree that granting new units to existing multi-unit franchisees is often a sound way to grow as they likely have the infrastructure in place, specifically related to people and structure, there still needs to be avenues where top-performing single-unit operators can expand their portfolio of locations. If this isn't the case, you may forever find yourself as a single-unit operator, and building your net worth may be exceedingly difficult if you can't grow past one location. It's worthwhile if you are keen to build a portfolio of locations to explore these decision-making criteria with your franchisor. Asking for specific examples of how the franchisor helped single-unit operators grow in the past is an excellent way to judge if that potential exists within the system today.

Trusted Expertise

The success of any business often hinges on its people, specifically their experience in a specialized field. The franchise world is no different. When exploring various franchised opportunities or trying to understand your own franchised system better, it's a good idea to explore two areas regarding the expertise within the system. First, how is relatable experience considered when bringing new franchisees on board? Second, how do departments at the franchisors' head office evaluate the relatable experience of new employees, and how do they continue to invest in developing their people after they join the organization?

Talented people help businesses thrive, and trusting that your franchisor focuses strongly on this area is integral to system success. Understanding how new franchisees are vetted into the system is a good idea. Great franchisors don't just look for net worth and access to capital before awarding new units; they also look for transferable skills that will help them operate their business. If your franchisor doesn't take this approach, you could find yourself a part of a system with franchisees who are unsuitable for the brand, which could put the success of the trade area and the franchised system as a whole in jeopardy.

The same can be said for how the franchisor hires and develops its employees, specifically those who work in departments that build programs, systems, and tools meant to support the franchisees and their business units, specifically operations, marketing, IT, and the design and construction teams. Given that so much of these departments' success will be determined by the strength of the leadership that oversees these areas, it's worthwhile to understand the biography of the executive team. What expertise do they have in their specific work function, and what leadership experience do they have? Employees today want to work for leaders who use an appreciative coaching style. Research shows that leaders who lead this way have lower employee turnover and build teams that continually learn and develop new skills [17], both areas that will dramatically impact franchisee success. Hiring operations, marketing, IT, or design and construction department employees with demonstrable experience and success in those areas is essential to franchisee success.

CHAPTER TWO

REFLECTIVE QUESTIONS

1. Does the franchisor share details about how the marketing funds are spent with the franchised system?

2. Do they also share details about how supplier rebates are managed?

3. How does the franchisor manage underperforming locations and franchisees within the system?

4. How does the franchisor vet potential franchisees to ensure they have the skills to run the business?

5. How does the franchisor ensure its senior executives and leaders hire the best available talent? How do those leaders continually invest in the coaching and development of their employees to mitigate damaging employee turnover?

NOTES & REFLECTIONS

CHAPTER THREE

Communication is the Cornerstone of Collaborative Success

Effective communication between key stakeholders is a cornerstone of successful collaboration [18]. People need to be able to talk with one another frequently to share information, knowledge, and ideas, which helps everyone move towards common goals. It's no less important in a franchised business environment but perhaps a little more difficult due to the complex nature of two interdependent systems working within the same organization – franchisees in their business units and employees working for the franchisor. Understanding how cross-functional communication practices in a franchised environment can help keep both groups informed and connected is essential. Equally important to the franchisee and franchisor's success is creating frequent opportunities to share feedback about how the franchise systems, programs, and tools are performing at the individual unit level.

So, what should you be looking for when assessing the effectiveness of the franchisor's communication tools and protocols? Let's dive in.

Role Clarity

For the franchise business model to thrive, franchisees need regular opportunities to have meaningful dialogue with the employees and leaders of the departments who create the programs, systems, and tools that support the franchise business model and, ultimately, the business units themselves. Franchisees need to be crystal clear on the avenues accessible to them to provide feedback and share their ideas regarding the business model and all the systems within it. To do that, they need to understand who does what within the franchisors' organization and have access to those folks so that their communication efforts can be successful.

A well-defined org chart with clearly established and defined job descriptions is crucial to achieving a healthy organization. People must know where they fit within the structure, what is expected of them in their day-to-day roles, and how that work contributes to the organization's overall success. It's a critical ingredient to cross-functional collaboration. Suppose the franchisees in the system don't understand who does what at the franchisors' head office and where to go when they have questions, especially in the departments that directly support the business operations. In that case, it can cause an information vacuum to develop, and in the absence of facts and data, assumptions grow and spread through the system. Departmental leaders need to ensure that franchisees and employees understand precisely what the various jobs within the department entail and whom franchisees can go to when they have comments, questions, or concerns. This one act alone can mitigate frustration between franchisees and the franchisor's employees, enhancing communication and building a more collaborative relationship.

Weekly Action Emails

The communication tool most utilized by franchisors is the weekly action email sent to the business units. When this tool is used effectively, it does an excellent job of keeping franchisees up to speed on the most important information for the upcoming week. The weekly email is often heavily weighted with input from the two departments most impacting the business units – marketing and operations. The best-in-class scenario is a joint weekly action email from both departments which ensures the operator needs only to look at one email for the week to get all the relevant information about what's happening in the system the following week. For example, if a new promotion starts, you should know exactly what is arriving in your point-of-sale marketing kit and when and where those assets need to go. It should also outline new or updated operational guidelines and other details to help operators unlock seamless execution at the individual business unit level. If your franchisor has an intranet, the direct links should be embedded into the weekly email where additional information or assets can be found so that you don't have to spend time scouring, often over-cluttered intranets for the information you need.

When marketing and operations jointly issue this communication, it makes it much easier for the franchisee to find the necessary information quickly. The communication also serves to ensure that the business units aren't going to experience 'initiative collision' whereby multiple initiatives are due to hit the business unit simultaneously, an absolute no-no when it comes to delivering seamless execution for your customers. The employee at the head office who manages the weekly action email process should also act as a gatekeeper to ensure this never happens. A final best practice to look for in these weekly emails is a 'whom to contact' section at the end. Giving franchisees access to who in each department they need to contact should they have questions or feedback is an excellent way to help the franchisor's employees build relationships at the franchisee level. It also serves to help franchisees know whom to go to instead of filtering all of their communication through their regional manager contact, as is typical in most franchised organizations.

Franchisee Surveys

Another communication tactic commonly used by the best franchisors to gauge the overall sentiments of their franchisees, specifically as it relates to the health of the franchisee/franchisor relationship, is to conduct an annual franchisee survey. Surveys are essential tools that measure franchisees' satisfaction with specific departments, their communication efforts, and their views on the overall system and its individual units' success. They also provide valuable benchmarking data that can be used to measure progress in these areas year-over-year. Measuring progress helps to ensure that any areas of the system or the relationships within that may have a low satisfaction score amongst the franchisee community are making meaningful progress towards overall enhancements. Like most things in business operations, what gets measured gets fixed.

Of course, completing an annual survey that measures the overall satisfaction of the franchisees is only half of the process. The franchisor must have a system in place that ensures each department reviews the franchisees' feedback and sentiments and works to make meaningful progress in enhancing any areas of opportunity. Asking for feedback from franchisees and then doing nothing with the information they provide is a surefire way to ensure the franchisees stop filling out the survey and offering feedback; this spells trouble for the entire system and should be avoided at all costs. Strong franchisors ensure that additional communication streams are successfully deployed after the annual survey has been completed, and all responses have been received.

First, systemwide communication is sent out, usually from the president of the franchised organization. This communication will highlight the areas franchisees identified as going well or as a strength for the system and, of course, the critical areas of opportunity and their next steps to address or further explore the issues raised. Second, a communication from each department head is issued, diving deeper into what's working within their scope of work and what needs to be explored further, potentially resulting in a different course of action.

Access to Senior Leaders

In most cases, franchisees will get all the relevant information related to what's most important in operating the business right now through detailed weekly communication from their regional manager or directly from the franchisors' operations and marketing teams, potentially through a communications department. However, this isn't always enough to ensure that franchisees feel heard. The franchisor needs to ensure that its senior leaders and executives are accessible to franchisees, especially if a significant or longstanding issue has yet to be resolved; this is where access to the departments' senior leaders becomes urgently important. I must point out here that when franchisees engage in conversations with senior leaders, executives, or any of the franchisors' employees, maintaining respect and composure during these conversations, especially when things are going wrong, is critical. I've been on the other end of conversations with franchisees that have been the opposite. When someone is yelling at you, using profanity, and generally taking their frustration out on you, it does not, quite obviously, promote healthy collaborative relationships. Respect and dignity for everyone are paramount to collective success.

One has to look no further than Popeyes Louisiana Kitchen under the leadership of then-CEO Cheryl Bachelder to understand how disengaged franchisees who have become frustrated with the system can impact everyone's results. Under Cheryl's leadership, the Popeyes corporate team adopted a servant leadership approach when working with their franchisees. Part of that approach entailed ensuring their senior leaders and executives were on deck when things went wrong. Listening carefully, especially when engaging with franchisees, was one of their six principles guiding how they worked together as part of one extensive system. The results of Cheryl's approach were nothing less than astounding, resulting in one of our time's greatest business turnaround stories. If you'd like to learn more about this particular example, I suggest picking up a copy of her book Dare to Serve; for me, it is an excellent example of how when franchisees and franchisors work collaboratively together towards a common goal, great things can happen.

Quarterly Franchisee Meetings

Another communication tactic commonly used to share upcoming business initiatives and results with franchisees are franchisor-led quarterly meetings held virtually, in-person, regionally, or as one large group. Signs of a collaborative quarterly meeting with your franchisor should include multiple opportunities for you to have a two-way dialogue, offer feedback, and engage in brainstorming sessions. Be on the lookout for quarterly meetings that are nothing more than a 'parade of PowerPoint' presentations, where the head of each department merely downloads the information they deem relevant to franchisees and nothing more. These meetings do little to build a collaborative working culture between franchisees and their franchisor. The same information could be sent in an email or a recorded webinar for franchisees to watch at their leisure. A broader business update followed by smaller round table sessions is much better suited to ensure meaningful collaboration with the system's franchisees takes place.

Franchisee Advisory Panels (FAC)

The final communication method we'll discuss commonly

used between franchisors and their franchisees is the establishment of a Franchisee Advisory Council (FAC). The FAC is a select group of franchisees that are asked to sit as a committee to meet frequently with the franchisor to discuss various elements of the business. Most often, the FAC help to gather feedback about proposed promotions, partnerships, or new product offerings while at the same time acting as representatives for specific geographies where they engage with the other franchisees in their area to collect their feedback for the purposes of sharing it back with the franchisor.

For the FAC to be an effective communication body for the system's franchisees, the franchisor must provide them with transparent and concise meeting minutes from each FAC meeting. These minutes should outline all the agreed-upon actions and next steps and a summary of the key discussions so that the FAC can share the information with their constituents. After all, these franchisees are business owners and operators, and asking them to take notes during meetings, type them up, and then share them with their region doesn't always work. The franchisor must do this for them. Ensuring this practice is in place serves another essential benefit for the system, not just saving time for the FAC representative. It also helps to avoid the game of telephone where a message starts one way and ends up as something entirely different when it reaches all franchisees. This type of broken communication can be very damaging to the franchised system.

Additionally, by providing communication for the FAC rep to send out to their region, the franchisor also avoids what I call 'selective sharing' by their FAC reps. Some members may deem certain information to be more important than other information, which can vary significantly across a large region or country, meaning that sharing information becomes inconsistent and certain franchisees in certain areas know certain things. Others are left in the dark creating information vacuums, which is also not a good result. So, when digging into your FAC, or inquiring about a potential franchisor's FAC practices, look specifically for how the franchisor manages the communication flow between the FAC members and their constituents.

Another benefit of the FAC is the ability to collect feedback from the system when needed. Frequent check-ins with franchisees can be very helpful when the franchisor needs a temperature check on new promotions, changes within the supply chain, or broader issues related to economic or political issues that may be impacting a specific region. The way the franchisor collects this feedback is critically important. Suppose they rely solely on hosting a meeting with the FAC and merely asking them to provide anecdotal input from their respective regions. In that case, the information they receive is likely to be biased based on the feelings of a particular FAC rep; this can be very dangerous for the franchisor, leaving a small group of personal feelings and beliefs to become too heavily weighted within the system. A better approach is to deploy a survey to the franchisees within each region, allowing them to communicate with their FAC rep and the franchisor directly. This survey data can supplement the information shared in the FAC meeting about the same topic. The franchisor must make all efforts to ensure that the data collected by the FAC reps and brought back to the franchisor accurately reflects how the collective region feels.

Effective communication between the franchisor and its franchisees is essential. Understanding how communication between these two groups is currently happening within your franchised system will indicate how much collaboration exists between them. Look for communication methods that are concise and transparent and offer opportunities for two-way feedback and dialogue. Communication like this will help to ensure everyone is moving together towards the common goal of franchisee success at the business unit level, as this always leads to franchisor success at the system level.

CHAPTER THREE

REFLECTIVE QUESTIONS

1. How does the franchisor ensure their franchisees know who does what in each department? Do franchisees know how problems should be escalated?

2. Does the franchisor send weekly communication to the business units sharing needed information about what's most important to the operations the following week?

3. Does the franchisor conduct an annual survey amongst the system's franchisees? Do they aim to understand their overall satisfaction with the business model and how they feel about their relationship with the franchisor? How do they act on the survey feedback?

4. Does the franchisor hold quarterly meetings with its franchisees? Are they a 'power-point parade', or do they engage in meaningful two-way dialogue?

5. How does the franchisor ensure that its executive team is accessible to the franchisees? Consider the last time the system faced a significant challenge; how did the executive team respond?

NOTES & REFLECTIONS

CHAPTER FOUR

How Marketing and Operations Impact Franchised Business Results

It's probably not a surprise to learn that the two departments within the franchisor's organization that have the most significant impact on your business are the marketing and operations teams. Understanding how these departments must work together to ensure maximum franchisee success is vital, as both groups have distinctly different responsibilities. Still, they rely on each other's contributions to be successful. This relationship isn't always easy; it's often the organizational area with the most friction between the working groups. In this chapter, we will explore why that is and what you'll see as a franchisee when these two groups work in lockstep to support you and your business results.

In traditional franchisor organizations, the marketing

department works to create programs and supporting materials that are used either nationally, regionally, or locally to help the franchised business units drive sales and increase customer visitation. When these tools and programs are built collaboratively with the operations department, there is an increased likelihood that execution at the business unit level will be enhanced. Therefore, the customer experience will likely be a positive one. When the opposite happens, and the marketing department works in a silo building these programs and their related materials, it's not uncommon for this approach to yield operational challenges. In my many years of working in the franchised environment, I have often experienced the results of marketing and operations departments working in silos and the negative impacts this has on the business units.

A lack of collaboration between these two departments often results in poor communication and a feeling that each unit is disconnected or out of touch. Ultimately, it's the franchisee that suffers. Organizational silos, specifically in these two departments, pose a significant risk to the business. When the left hand doesn't know what the right hand is doing, this lack of collaboration fuels a lack of innovation [19], resulting in poor operational execution at the business unit level. So, why does this happen? Why do these two groups specifically often end up siloed off in many organizations? Well, it has much to do with the different worldviews of marketing and operations professionals, not unlike the differences between entrepreneurs and those who choose the corporate career path. Understanding these different worldviews is essential to enhancing how they work together to support the franchisees. Let's take a closer look.

Marketing and operations professionals are unique groups of individuals. While marketing folks tend to see the world from a revenue growth and brand positioning perspective, working hard to influence consumers with their new programs to drive increased traffic and sales, operations folks are somewhat different. Operations professionals see the world from an execution, compliance, and cost containment perspective. They continually look for ways to maximize profitability while maintaining a strong focus on the day-to-day execution of the brand standards and customer experience. These differing world views promote the polarity between marketing and operations professionals within a franchised system. When is it the right time to focus on driving sales and customer growth, and have those initiatives been designed to enable consistent execution at the business unit level? When is it the right time to focus on profitability and the execution of brand standards because signals suggest the business is not operating as it should be?

Understanding this polarity within the franchisor's organization is vital because both departments and their work are essential to ensuring that the business achieves maximum success and profitability. Unfortunately, for those looking for a quick fix to this problem, there isn't one; by definition, polarities are problems that can't be solved [20]. Instead, they need to be managed. Senior leaders and executives within the franchisor's organization need to help both groups get the best work out of each other while minimizing the limiting factors that result from a singular focus on marketing or a singular focus on operations. This is why the relationship between these two departments is critical to your franchised locations' success. So, what will you see as a franchisee when these departments work collaboratively to help drive your business results? When trying to understand how well or not your franchisor's marketing and operations departments are working together, there are three signals to be on the lookout for. First, how well do individuals in these departments understand their *departmental interdependencies*, how much time do both departments' team members spend *working in the business units*, and finally, do they *share common goals* linked to franchisee success? Let's take a closer look at each of these signals.

Understanding Departmental Interdependencies

When senior leaders in the marketing and operations departments understand the interdependency in the success of each department's initiatives, it opens the door for more opportunities to collaborate and share ideas, best practices, and invaluable feedback that ultimately benefits the entire system. Once the employees in both the marketing and operations departments understand all the roles in each other's work areas and how they contribute to franchisee success, they must have meaningful opportunities to collaborate in any shared areas linked to the business operations. Hosting joint meetings is a vital tactic needed to unlock that collaboration, specifically in two areas: ideation of new marketing programs for the business units and a post-mortem on these programs after they launch in the field.

Marketing the business is essential to franchisee success and strong unit economics, but only if the programs and initiatives developed are built with ease of consistent execution across the system in mind. Suppose these initiatives are too complex and can't be executed well or consistently across the system. In that case, it harms the business instead, as ultimately, the customer experience suffers, damaging the brand and the unit economics. This is why joint meetings between marketing and operations during the ideation phase are so critical; they can highlight any operational issues before the launch and get the operations team involved in solving those issues, ultimately creating a better experience for customers and frontline staff.

Similarly, hosting joint meetings post-launch of new programs and initiatives is also essential for franchisee success. As the operations team is in the field supporting the business units during a new launch, early issues are flagged, while at the same time, franchisees and their employees develop new best practices. Ensuring these issues are discussed collaboratively to be solved and actioned in real-time is paramount to consistent execution and a strong customer experience. Additionally, nearly all best practices related to operational execution come from the employees working on the frontlines. The franchisor's operations team must spot these best practices early in new launches and initiatives, discuss them at cross-functional meetings, and then share them broadly with the entire system so that every business unit and its customers can benefit. In part two of this book, we'll talk more about the importance of the franchisor having a robust system and process for adopting and sharing best practices, as it's a critical part of achieving a consistent customer experience for the brand.

Experience Life in the Business Units

The two departments with the most significant impact on franchisee success should be familiar with what life at the frontlines of the business is like, as it's for the frontline staff that they are building and enhancing the systems' operational programs and tools. Not only will the feedback they receive by spending time with the business units as they serve their customers help them enhance existing programs, systems, and tools, but it's also an essential part of providing franchisee support and relationship building. Having employees experience what life is like in each other's departments' day-to-day work is an excellent way to create the necessary understanding of how that work impacts each other and the franchisee. This strategy can also shed light on the need for standardized processes that help support the adoption and execution of the programs, systems, and tools used to drive business results. While it may be daunting for the employees of the marketing team to spend time in the business units, doing so with an employee of the operations team can make it feel less so. Valuable lessons and experiences can develop when we see the many complexities in each role, and that understanding makes collaboration easier and more effective.

The system has three main benefits when franchisors' employees spend time in the business units observing the operations, providing training, or offering support. The first benefit is that marketing and operations employees will see how their programs, systems, and tools perform at the business unit level. Face-to-face interaction between these distinct groups allows them to review current or new procedures and initiatives, ask questions and seek solutions to any problems that may be bubbling up from the frontline employees. It's also important to note that when the senior executives who direct the operations and marketing departments do not spend time in the field, they risk detaching themselves from the day-to-day operations. They simultaneously lose insight into the effectiveness of their department's programs and tools used to drive traffic and support the frontline staff.

The second benefit to the franchised system when employees of both the marketing and operations departments spend time in the field with the franchisees and their teams has to do with innovation. By changing your physical surroundings and opening your eyes and ears to what you see and hear that is different from your normal day-to-day activities, you expose yourself to new perspectives and ideas from those who work at the frontlines of the business every day. Innovation often results when the franchisor increases the time its employees are exposed to life at the business unit level and the challenges they face. These experiences are critical to the success of franchisees and the franchisor, as innovative ideas and solutions are often required at the system level to respond to environmental pressures and market challenges.

In contrast to this approach, when employees of the marketing and operations departments don't step out of their departments to evaluate, and stress test their ideas, the franchisor's exposure to groupthink rises, thereby diminishing opportunities to collaborate and innovate with the franchisees and their employees. Groupthink is dangerous to any organization as it leads people to set aside doubts or concerns and make decisions without critically testing, analyzing, and evaluating all possible options. Instead of having an open discussion with the people that use their programs, systems, and tools, which is essential to collaborative problem-solving and creativity, the employees of the franchisor stay in a closed-loop environment and yield to the temptation to minimize conflict and reach a consensus instead of challenging each other's ideas and rationale.

Another benefit to the franchised system when employees from both marketing and operations spend time in the field relates to how the franchisor collects and evaluates data. Immersing oneself in the operations at the business unit level is a valuable way for the franchisor to observe and gather data on the performance of the business model. Business unit-level observation allows the employees of these departments to compare everything they see and hear about the business model while working on the frontlines with what they may have interpreted from other data sources.

Including business unit-level observational data with more traditional data collection methods such as historical reporting data and conducting surveys or questionnaires could enhance the validity of the franchisor's process to evaluate the programs, systems, and tools used to operate the business. Whenever the results from several different data collection methods are aligned and highlight the same patterns and themes, you can be more confident that the results represent a more accurate indication of the problem being evaluated or the 'root cause,' so to speak. Data collected from business unit-level observation can be a powerful tool in the franchisors' arsenal when assessing the business model's effectiveness and considering the capabilities of potential new programs and tools.

Common Goals

Without a doubt, the marketing and operations

departments within the franchisor's organization significantly impact the franchised units' business model and, ultimately, the franchisees' success. Ensuring that both departments share the common goal of increasing same-unit sales growth and are actively and collectively working towards that goal is critically important. Driving operationally sound same-unit sales growth for the franchisee is crucial to ensuring the system achieves profitable unit economics. Remember, franchisees are entrepreneurs who go into business to make a profit, and healthy unit economics cannot be overstated. Similarly, the franchisor also needs strong unit economics to sell more locations, thus increasing brand exposure in developing markets.

The marketing department of most franchisors works hard to develop new programs, promotions, and advertising materials used to promote the brand and drive traffic into the individual business units. At the same time, the operations department works on how these programs and promotions must be executed to live up to the brand standards, ensuring that customers are satisfied with what could be their first experience with the brand. Both aspects of this work are equally important in driving sales and profitability for the franchisee; as we discussed in chapter one, if you were to separate these workflows, only focusing on either driving sales or operational execution, the overall business would suffer. These two groups share a significant interdependency that is essential to the success of individual franchisees and the system.

CHAPTER FOUR

REFLECTIVE QUESTIONS

1. Do the operations and marketing departments have shared business goals related to franchisees' success?

2. Do these departments regularly meet to discuss innovation, execution, and initiative results?

3. Do the marketing and operations department employees spend time in the franchised business units seeking feedback about their programs, systems, and tools?

4. How do the marketing and operations executives stay connected to life at the frontlines of the business?

NOTES & REFLECTIONS

PRINCIPLE TWO

Consistency is What Makes a Franchised System Successful

CHAPTER FIVE

Consistent Execution of Brand Standards is Required for Franchisee Success

One of the main reasons entrepreneurs invest in buying a franchised business is the well-designed operating system that has proven successful in the minds of customers and operators alike. Opening your own, non-franchised business comes with substantial risk around your ability to design an operating system that works and your continued ability to evaluate and update that system as the business environment and your customers' expectations change. Investing in a franchise with a well-qualified team of professionals whose sole focus is the programs, systems, and tools required to operate the business is the driving force behind why many entrepreneurs end up in the franchised world.

As a franchised operations professional, I've always

found it curious why franchisees would invest their money and time into buying a franchise with a proven operating system and then fail to follow the franchisor's brand standards; it doesn't make much sense to me. If the system has proved successful and evolved into a franchise, not trusting the methods that helped it become successful seems counterintuitive. Yet, I saw it repeatedly across several franchised systems. One of the most important things you can do as a franchisee is to dedicate as much time as is required to knowing your brand standards inside and out. What are the necessary steps to deliver a customer experience that will keep people coming back repeatedly, helping you build a solid reputation in your community?

Most successful franchises have operations manuals, job aids, training materials, and in some cases, training teams that outline their brand standards and service expectations step by step. It's your job as a franchisee to know them inside and out and to ensure that your employees are executing them consistently across all the dayparts your business is open. Failing to perform this one critical step will jeopardize your customer experience, community reputation, and ability to run a profitable business. It will also jeopardize the brand's reputation and the investment and capital of every franchisee within the system.

Franchisors take this commitment to brand standards very seriously. One needs only to look at the franchise agreement to see the penalty for franchisees who breach this part of the contract. It's common for the franchisor to have the ability to de-brand your business, taking down the trademarks, marketing material, and all content related to how the business model operates should you repeatedly fail to execute the brand standards consistently. There are usually three main methods a franchisor will use to monitor execution at the business unit level: *operations assessments*, *customer feedback programs*, and *third-party quality assurance audits*. Let's take a look at each one a bit closer.

Operations Assessments

Most large franchisors employ a team of regional managers whose primary function is to monitor the performance of the business units in their region. Depending on the franchisors' expectations and the size of the regional managers' region, you can expect at least one, if not two, complete operations assessments each year. These assessments usually entail the regional manager spending a full day in your business unit observing how customers are serviced according to the brand standards. They may also look closely at things like cleanliness, adherence to marketing programs, and the repair and maintenance of core equipment needed to execute the business model. These visits may be announced and scheduled with the franchisee, or they may not, or they may be a combination of both. Regardless, the best advice here is to act as if every day is assessment day. If you take this approach, you'll consistently score well, which ensures you take great care of your customers and maintain a positive relationship with your regional manager and, ultimately, the franchisor.

The results generated by these operations assessments are an important tool your franchisor will use to measure the entire system's health. Overall solid results across the system indicate that operations are running smoothly and that compliance with the brand standards is high. Results like this suggest to the franchisor that the system could handle additional complexity through new and innovative products or extra sales volume through added promotional activity. Both are good things when it comes to driving sales. When the system scores are low overall on operations assessments, it can indicate to the franchisor that certain parts of the customer experience have become too complex and challenging to execute, potentially requiring a different method or new approach. Regardless of the outcome, these tools deliver essential information to the franchisor about the overall consistency of execution, which helps inform their business planning approach.

Customer Feedback

Another common approach used to measure the consistency of the customer experience is implementing mechanisms that look at service from two perspectives, the first being your online reputation. The second is a more detailed service assessment at the individual customer level. Let's look at online reputation first.

Several tools exist that automate collecting your business units' various online reviews. These tools work in such a way that they automatically collect all your customer feedback daily from websites like Google, Yelp, Trip Advisor, Facebook, and many other platforms that may be relevant to your specific industry. These tools automate the delivery of a summary of the feedback these platforms generate to you, the operator, and usually to the regional manager overseeing your location. The best operators know that this feedback is essential to enhancing your overall operations and take it seriously, implementing actions immediately to correct any issues. They also know that the higher their star rating is on these sites, the more business they will drive to their establishment, enhancing their topline sales and, ultimately, their profit. A recent study by Womply, a digital-first organization that helps small businesses on main street thrive in the digital age, found that small businesses like restaurants, retailers, salons, and auto shops with a star rating of between 4 and 4.5 had, on average, 28% higher sales than those establishments with lower star ratings. Their study of over 200,000 US small businesses also revealed that the number of reviews your business has matters significantly, with companies with less than 85 reviews attaining 15% less revenue than those with 85 reviews or more [21]. So, if your business consistently receives negative customer feedback and has an overall star rating lower than the brand's average, expect to be on the radar of your regional manager and franchisor.

Another common way franchisors collect feedback about the overall customer experience is to use either guest surveys or mystery shoppers. Both tools allow the franchisor to audit various aspects of the service experience in more detail. These tools benefit both the franchisor and the franchisee as the feedback is very specific and detailed, enabling you to take definitive action and correct that part of the customer experience. This feedback is also important to the franchisor, allowing them to see across the system where operators have difficulty executing to standard. They then can look at how the standard is meant to be performed and make alterations to ease the process or provide additional training tools or job aides to help enhance execution which is a win-win for all. Failure to serve your customers in line with the brand standards jeopardizes your and the entire system's reputation, so these infractions are not often tolerated.

Third-Party Quality Assurance

The final method a franchisor might use to evaluate the overall consistency of their business units won't apply to all franchised systems as this type of evaluation is most commonly used when there are parts of the operating system that, when not followed exactly as the standard is written can result in significant harm to either the business units employees or customers. Third-party quality assurance is standard in the hospitality industry, as foodborne illness is a critical concern. Should issues arise, people's lives could be at risk, jeopardizing the entire brand's reputation. One need only look at the Jack-in-the-Box food safety issue that impacted over 700 individuals, killing ten and seriously injuring almost 200 in 1992 and 1993 [22].

Third-party quality assurance audits are almost exclusively unannounced to the business unit. These assessments aim to understand how the business operates on any given day. They are usually very detailed, especially regarding food safety, and will likely take several hours to complete. The assessors will look closely at your food handling processes from when a product enters your building from a distributor to how it is prepped, stored, and ends up on the customers' plate. Infractions are not tolerated and can result in the immediate closure of your business if numerous violations are found. Franchisors take these reports very seriously; if you historically perform below the system's average in these assessments, expect heightened scrutiny from not only your regional manager but also the senior leaders within the operations department.

One of the main reasons for investing in a franchise is to obtain a tried and tested operating system that delivers a solid customer experience and builds profitable sales. Your commitment as a franchisee to the consistent execution of those brand standards is a commitment you will be required to make. If you aren't prepared to do so, owning a franchise is not for you. The franchisor often treats repeated infractions in this area in the most serious of ways, as it's their primary responsibility to protect the brand and the investment of every other franchisee within the system.

CHAPTER FIVE

REFLECTIVE QUESTIONS

1. What training tools and processes does the franchisor have to help you consistently execute the brand standards?

2. Does the franchisor regularly conduct operational assessments in the business units? What is the average score in the system? Is it improving?

3. How does the franchisor monitor the social media scores and customer reviews for the entire system? What's the average star rating across the various review platforms?

4. Does the franchisor use a third-party organization to monitor and assess the critical safety elements for staff and customers? What is the average system score? Have there been significant issues identified in the past? How were those issues resolved?

NOTES & REFLECTIONS

CHAPTER SIX

Consistently Executed Training Leads to Consistent Operations

Trying to achieve consistency in your operations without adherence to a standardized training program for your managers and staff will be next to impossible. In my career, I've often witnessed franchisees who try to cut corners on training costs, putting people into positions without adequate training time, only to see the negative impacts this has on team morale and the customer experience. Simply put, this is one business area you cannot sacrifice if you want to operate according to brand standards and consistently exceed your customers' expectations. Taking full advantage of your franchisor's training opportunities and tools is essential to success. Let's look at the three most common training opportunities franchisors provide: *new franchisee training*, *positional training paths*, and *franchisor-led training teams*. Let's dive in.

New Franchisee Training

The best franchisors know that showing new franchisees what right looks like as it relates to the operations of the business model is essential to their brand's success. A learning approach like this often comes in an immersive on-the-job training experience ranging from several weeks to several months, depending on the brand and the complexity of its operations. The training will either occur in a franchised location that consistently ranks amongst the chain's top performers or at a franchisor-owned and operated site. Regardless of who conducts the training, corporate or franchised employees, getting the absolute most out of this experience is vital to your success.

One of the most significant missed opportunities related to new franchisee training is that the new franchisees don't bring their key staff to participate, most likely due to additional costs. It cannot be overstated how valuable it is to have at least one or two of your key personnel join you, especially if you will not be directly responsible for the day-to-day business management, turning that responsibility over to a general manager. You'll have so much to think about once you take over your business or open its doors for the first time that this dedicated time for your learning and development will be challenging to duplicate back in the 'real world,' so to speak. So, leverage this opportunity to take as many key staff members as the economics and franchisor will allow. Trust me when I say it's an investment that pays back tenfold when striving to achieve strong execution when opening day/take-over day arrives.

Another missed opportunity I have often seen related to new franchisee training is the need for more commitment and focus on the training once it begins. While I can certainly appreciate that life is busy and there are competing priorities leading up to takeover or grand opening day, you will not get this dedicated time to build a strong foundation of understanding related to the business model again. Trying to manage emails, phone calls, and other distractions takes away from the experience, and it shows a lack of commitment to the individuals training you and the franchisor, which is not a great start. The other consideration is to those other new franchisees who may be attending the same training sessions as you. Your constant distractions disrupt the entire class, so make plans to disconnect and focus on learning as much as possible throughout the training experience.

When considering the purchase of a franchise, understanding their process for training new franchisees and if there is an opportunity to bring key staff with you is essential. New franchisee training will set the foundation for understanding how the business model operates and familiarize you with the systems and tools required to train the employees when your location opens.

Franchisor-Led Training Teams

It's common when opening a new franchised location built from the ground up to have an 'opening team' that consists of either trainers who work for the franchisor, top-performing employees from neighboring franchisees, or a combination of both to support you in the opening of your new business. These training teams are deployed to your new location to ensure that the new employees you have hired are trained from day one according to brand standards. Coupled with the foundational knowledge you learned during your new franchisee training program, this is a powerful starting position for you as a new franchisee.

It would be best if you considered hiring a full complement of employees and managers to maximize the time the opening training team spends at your location; in fact, some franchisors will mandate this. Having as many new employees participate in this training as possible right from day one will ensure your new business opens to customers on the right foot, with solid execution. Remember, you have only one chance to make a first impression in your community. Customers will have some tolerance for minor missteps during your first week or two of operations, but that tolerance will soon fade. Once the training team leaves, the consistent execution of the brand standards rests solely on you and your employees. Your foundation will be stronger by ensuring you have a full roster of employees hired and available for training.

Similar to understanding what the new franchisee training program entails, it is equally important to understand what kind of training and support the franchisor offers when opening a brand-new location compared to buying an existing unit from an existing franchisee. In my experience, it is often the latter situation, buying an existing unit, that comes with the least amount of support on the take-over day.

Positional Training Paths

Once you've opened your new location or taken over an existing unit that was for sale, your business's ongoing training rests solely on you, the franchisee. The best franchisors understand the risk to the brand by letting franchisees create their own training programs and tools; the negative impact this has on brand consistency cannot be overstated. That's why experienced franchisors offer detailed training paths for every position it takes to operate the business.

These training paths and tools may vary by the franchisor, but be on the lookout for training programs that offer a blend of online learning through the franchisor's intranet or another online learning tool and a detailed on-the-job training program that happens over several days for the new employee. Adults learn in several key ways, some by reading, some by observing, and some by doing. Franchisors that understand this have usually built a training program incorporating training elements that use each style. Experienced franchisors will also often audit your training practices to assess your compliance with the brand's training standards, as solid training is the foundation for consistent execution.

Experienced franchisors also know that the leaders who run the business units will determine the culture in which the franchisee's employees come to work every day. To help the franchisee avoid costly turnover, which negatively impacts the overall unit economics, and to protect the franchisee's employer brand and the franchisor's image, they often offer a specific training path for managers. A good manager training path focuses on leadership that builds a strong culture that treats the business's employees with respect and dignity. This type of training is essential to your business's success as labor markets across North America are challenged to hire entry-level workers. Employing leaders in your business that don't create the ideal working culture means you will likely lose out on hiring the best available talent to the competition.

Understanding what training programs and tools your franchisor or a potential franchisor has to offer is critical. These tools and programs will help you ensure the adequate training of employees and managers, which is paramount to your success. Of course, understanding what those tools and programs are isn't enough. You must embrace those training paths and tools in your business to ensure that everyone who comes to work for you has a consistent training experience that delivers a solid understanding of what right looks like and how the business is meant to operate. Failure to do so will ultimately leave you with poor execution, disappointed customers, high employee turnover, and a concerned franchisor, none of which are good business outcomes.

CHAPTER SIX

REFLECTIVE QUESTIONS

1. How does the franchisor train new franchisees in the system?

2. How does the franchisor support staff training in new unit openings?

3. How does the franchisor support a seamless transition in re-sale situations from one franchisee to another?

4. Does the franchisor have detailed training paths for staff and managers with supporting tools and processes for each position needed to operate the business?

5. How does the franchisor support the training of business unit leaders?

6. How does the franchisor incorporate the three adult learning styles into its training curriculums?

NOTES & REFLECTIONS

CHAPTER SEVEN

How Franchisors Manage 'Best Practices' is Critical to Consistent Execution

One of the most challenging things for any organization to manage are the 'best practices' that come out of the operations in each business unit. It's inevitable that when the organization builds programs, systems, and tools in a corporate office for use in the business units, these same programs, systems, and tools will be enhanced or changed in some way by the people who use them every day. There is no use in the franchisor trying to stop this from happening. The best approach for the system and the brand is to implement processes that bubble these best practices up to the head office so that they can be evaluated, tested, and, if warranted, launched into the entire system so that all operators can benefit.

So, what should you look for to see how best practices are

being managed in your franchise system or a franchise you are exploring? First, be on the lookout for how new programs, systems, and tools are initially developed; a collaborative approach between the franchisor's team and the employees at the frontlines of the business can lead to a lesser need from the system to have to alter these programs, systems, and tools in the first place. Second, look for specific communication avenues that enable sharing new best practices with the franchisor's team. Innovation is vital to business continuity and can be very powerful when it comes from the frontlines, so celebrating innovation and making it easy to share ideas with meaningful two-way communication is essential. Finally, look at how best practices are conveyed back to the system and made into new operating standards; this will show you how well the franchisor listens and reacts when new and enhanced ways of completing existing tasks are created. Let's take a closer look at each of these areas.

Developing New Programs, Systems, and Tools

One of the most important tools at the franchisors' disposal regarding how best practices are managed within the system is how new programs, systems, and tools are created in the first place. A collaborative approach involving franchisees and their operations teams early and often is crucial for building the right tools that the business can quickly adopt. The franchisor needs to unlock three key collaborative efforts for this process to happen: designing the program, testing the program, and the continuing evaluation of the program. Let's look at each stage a little closer.

Involving the people that will use the new program, system, or tool in the design phase is critical to adoption. After all, the people using these tools day in and day out often have the best perspective on how it should be created, and the best franchisors know this. A process that actively solicits input from those working on the frontlines is critical to making this collaboration happen. Whether that collaboration comes from a selected group of the best-operated business units or business units specified by each regional manager, the point is to ensure that there is a way to engage the frontlines in a way that harnesses the collective innovation and expertise of this group.

Early collaboration with field operations is a critical first step; the entire system pays the price when it doesn't happen. Restaurant franchisees reading this book will likely have heard the phrase 'what the heck were they thinking when they created this menu item" from their staff working in the kitchen. Chances are every restaurant back-of-house team member has uttered this at least once in their lives. Feelings like this emerge when new menu items are designed without first checking the process in a location during peak sales revenue. Trust me when I say you want to be part of a franchised system that collaborates with field operations up front in the design process of any new program, system, or tool used in the business.

Capturing Best-Practices from the Field

One of the most critical questions a franchisor can ask themselves regarding the best practices generated in the field is how easy it is for the employees working in the business units or the franchisor's field operations team to share their innovative ideas. An overly complex process will ensure these ideas never reach the right people working in the franchisor's head office who can decide to explore the concept further or shut it down. The best franchisors use at least two methods to gather these new best practices from the field. First, a dedicated email address where employees from the business units can send their ideas, photos, and videos. And second, a process for regional managers to follow when they stumble across these ideas while out in the field.

A dedicated email address is the most effective. Employees from the field can shoot a quick video or take a series of photos accompanying the best practice right from their phone and send it off to the franchisor's head office. It's fast and easy without a lot of 'red tape,' which can deter frontline employees from sharing their innovations with the head office. Whether it be a new menu item, service enhancement, or local marketing promotion, the best franchisors have dedicated individuals who monitor these best practice emails and send them to the appropriate department. Look for an automated email that arrives immediately after the best practice has been sent, giving the employee peace of mind that the email has been received and is going to the right team. Of course, follow-up from the correct department is essential; they'll want to know what will happen next and how the idea will be evaluated. More on that a bit later.

Another process commonly used by franchisors to collect best practices from the field is to unlock a straightforward way for their regional managers to share the best practices they observe when visiting locations in their regions. Instead of asking the employee in the business unit to submit their best practices, which they may feel uncomfortable doing, the regional managers can detail the best practice on their behalf and then submit that information directly to a senior operations leader for their perspective. If there is alignment that the idea is good, it makes its way to the senior leaders in the appropriate department for their thoughts and feedback. It's quick and easy for the regional managers to capture and share the information and get it into the hands of the right people in the right departments.

I cannot overstate the importance of franchisors collecting innovative ideas from their system; to assume that good ideas only come from the head office is a mistake and represents a franchisor who is out of touch with those who operate the business every day. The employees who work daily at the frontlines of the business often have identified challenges in the system long before someone at the head office even knows there is a problem. Making it easy for them to share their solutions and ideas is critical. In restaurants specifically, the best kitchen and menu innovations often come from the folks who work with the approved ingredients daily. Tapping into their ideas is a terrific way to provide your guests with menu innovation using ingredients and equipment already existing in the operating system.

Adopting Best-Practices Within the System

The final piece of the best practice puzzle is the most important, as it directly impacts the consistency of the brand experience for all customers. One of the main reasons franchises become so successful is that they train their customers to expect the same product or service from them at any location they visit. McDonald's is an excellent example; it may not be the best hamburger in the world, but it looks and tastes the same no matter where you eat it. Protecting this consistency for customers is why franchisors must have a process for dealing with best practices that deviate from the standard operating procedure. Unique innovations and enhanced ways of doing things can come from a franchised system, but ultimately the product and service offering has to be consistent across the chain. It's that consistency that's built loyalty with the customers, so ensuring that there is a well-established practice for vetting best practices and either updating the standard for the whole system or disallowing the new approach to provide a consistent customer experience is vital. In my franchise history, this element of managing best practices is the most difficult to execute as no one likes being the bad guy saying no to someone else's idea. Still, it's crucial to maintain that consistent brand experience.

The best franchisors manage this potential issue by having an established process for vetting best practices. They transparently share that process with franchisees and then honor it as best practices and innovation emerge from the field. There are several different ways this vetting process can take place; the most effective is when the franchisor has the appropriate department look at the benefits or enhancements the new practice offers to the business model. Does it enhance the speed of service or the overall customer experience? Does it strengthen profitability or provide additional ways to drive revenue? If the answer is yes, the logical next step is for the franchisor to understand if the new practice is scalable, meaning, will it work in every business unit across the system? This is often where the rubber hits the road from a vetting standpoint.

I've seen much innovation come from franchisees trying to meet the needs of their customers in a specific region or market, and this is a tricky spot for the franchisor to be in. Do you allow variations of products and services based on geography, or do you stick to a standardized set of offerings to maintain customer consistency? Not an easy position to be in. It becomes somewhat more manageable when the innovation is related to new best practices that enhance the execution of an existing standard, process, or tool. Suppose frontline employees devise a way to enhance a current procedure that still delivers the same, or better, quality of product or service but in a more streamlined and faster way. In that case, testing it out in multiple locations makes sense to ensure it's viable in all sale volumes. If the test has a favorable outcome, the entire system can benefit from that new procedure.

It is important to understand how your franchisor or potential franchisor handles collecting and vetting best practices and innovations from the field to see if they are scalable across the system. It will give you a good insight into how they collaborate with their franchisees when it comes to the operations of the business. The regionality of the products and services is a trickier conversation. I've seen franchisees in various brands get very enthusiastic about having regional offerings, and at the end of the day, it comes from a good place, a place of wanting to serve their customers well. Still, this can quickly get out of hand from the franchisor's perspective. I'd suggest asking how these conversations have been handled in the past, as it will be a good indicator of how they might address them in the future.

CHAPTER SEVEN

REFLECTIVE QUESTIONS

1. Does the franchisor work with the frontline employees in the business units to design new products, systems, and tools?

2. How do the frontline employees share their feedback and best practices with the franchisor?

3. How does the franchisor evaluate new ideas and best practices from the frontlines?

4. How does the franchisor share best practices with the entire system?

5. How has the franchisor previously handled requests for regional variations in products or services?

NOTES & REFLECTIONS

CHAPTER EIGHT

Consistent Local Marketing Efforts Enhance Unit Economics

Aside from running solid operations that deliver a consistent customer experience, consistently marketing your business as a franchisee is one of the best things you can do to drive healthy unit economics. Unfortunately, in my experience, marketing is also one of the areas I've seen franchisees struggle with the most, as having a marketing background isn't a prerequisite to becoming a franchisee in most brands. In this chapter, I hope to highlight the most successful local and regional marketing efforts I've seen deployed at the franchisee level. Specifically, how to amplify your franchisor's national marketing efforts and local marketing strategies that work to promote your brand during your off-peak business periods; let's take a closer look.

Amplifying National Promotions Locally

As we discussed in part one of this book, it's very common in the franchised world for franchisors to collect a marketing fee on behalf of the franchisees in the system. The fee can range from 1% to 4.5% and is used collectively to promote the brand and drive customers to your business. The best franchisors have their marketing efforts for the calendar year mapped out in advance and proactively share that calendar with their franchisees so that they, too, can plan their marketing efforts for the year ahead. The best franchisees understand that when the franchisor has planned a marketing initiative that includes a strong brand presence on TV, radio, and billboards, focusing your efforts on the same promotion locally will enhance your results. This is not the time to run a competing local offer that could confuse your customers and drive up your promotional discount line on the P&L.

If you want to further market your business during a national promotion to make an even more significant impact, consider buying additional local radio or TV placements to increase local awareness. Or better yet, investing in your operations and scheduling additional employees to ensure that execution is the best it can be during this time of increased traffic is money well spent. I can't tell you how often I've seen franchisees layer on offer after offer while the franchisor promotes a national promotion. This is costly to the discount line and confusing for customers. Your best bet is to double down on the national advertising locally to drive as much customer traffic as possible with only one discounted offer.

As a franchisee, once you determine your additional marketing spend for the upcoming fiscal year, plan to meet with a member of the marketing department to discuss their forthcoming marketing calendar so that you can align your investment to make the best impact locally. I've worked with some franchisors who have preemptively shown the marketing calendar in regional or national franchisee meetings. Still, these meetings won't always align with your business planning time, and the franchisor won't always share the year's calendar at once. It's more common to share the upcoming quarters' marketing plans which, with a bit of planning and discussion on your part, can work just as well. If you plan to spend an additional 1% of sales on local marketing efforts, determine the dollar value and set a budget for each quarter. When you work with local radio, TV, and digital media partners, you can often get a better deal when buying a year's worth of advertising upfront but offering up the creative on a campaign-by-campaign basis. Before deciding to create costly ads with an external agency, always check with your franchisor first. I've often seen it be the case where the franchisors' creative has been shared with the franchisees saving a significant amount of time and budget. Sharing resources allows the franchisee to buy more digital impressions or TV and radio time while ensuring that the marketing content has the same look and feel whether the customer sees it on a national or local platform. This strategy goes a long way to promote a consistent brand message with a consistent look and feel.

Local Marketing Programs That Work

Over the years, I've seen the good, the bad, and the ugly related to franchisees' local marketing efforts. Local marketing can hugely impact your business results when done right and not in conflict with national promotions designed by the franchisor with your marketing dollars. The best franchisees understand that less is more regarding their local efforts and that a consistent approach is required to build customer loyalty. Choosing your programs carefully and then letting them gain traction over time is necessary to succeed at the local marketing level.

One of the biggest reasons franchisees look to do additional marketing in their communities is to drive sales on specific days of the week with less traffic. This approach can be highly successful if you pick the right offer. Where I've seen franchisees be unsuccessful in these efforts is not because of the offer itself but because of a lack of effort or knowledge of how to promote the offer within the community. Failing to reach outside your four walls to create awareness in the neighborhood means you'll most likely discount customers already coming to your business. Not a good marketing strategy.

Reaching into your franchisee community to learn from their experience regarding what offers work to drive traffic is a great tactic. One of the many benefits of being in a franchised system is that you have a wealth of knowledge and experience at your fingertips, don't be afraid to use it and learn from their successes and failures. Whatever you do to drive new customers to your business, choose a compelling yet profitable offer, and then get out into the community to promote that offer. Consider a social media strategy to supplement your boots-on-the-ground efforts hitting various businesses, schools, etc., to spread the word and remember that these initiatives often take time to build a following, so consistency with your efforts is essential. Stopping and starting promotions without giving them time to drive new customers is one of the worst things you can do to build loyalty. Take your time, choose the right offer and daypart, then hunker down to do the work; over time, you'll build a successful marketing campaign.

The next challenge will be to understand when it's the right time to end the promotion; after all, if you continue to discount a product or service over a long period, you eventually decrease the perceived value of the product or service in the eyes of your customers. Leaning on the expertise of your franchisor's marketing team to help you make this decision is one way to approach the timing of your offers. The other way is to track your sales and redemptions with great discipline. Tracking how well your local marketing efforts perform weekly is how you gain critical insight into which promotions are working and building over time and which promotions may not be gaining traction and should end.

Once your promotions have been gaining traction week over week, and you've succeeded in driving business to other dayparts or slower days, it's time to think about discontinuing the offer and then evaluating, post-promotion, how those same dayparts or days of the week perform. Do you see a lift in sales and traffic post-promotion compared to pre-promotion? How are your overall weekly sales and customer counts post-promotion compared to pre-promotion? If these metrics increase, you're doing an excellent job within your community to grow your business; if not, it's time to return to the drawing board. Tracking your metrics is critical; if you ignore the results of your efforts, how will you know if your actions are working? You may be discounting customers for the sake of discounting, which is never good for unit economics.

One final word on how to market your business consistently in the community; whatever you choose to do from the program or promotion perspective, discuss your plan with your regional manager or your franchisor's marketing department. You'll want to ensure that any content you use on social media or for any posters and flyers you may consider making to support your efforts is in line with your brand's marketing standards. Most brands use specific fonts, colors, and images to promote the brand nationally. Using something that doesn't meet the marketing style guidelines of your franchisor's national marketing efforts delivers an inconsistent brand message to customers, the opposite of what strong brands try to do. So don't miss this step when designing the assets for your local marketing initiatives, as franchisor approval is often required to ensure consistent trademarks and branding. Failing to secure approval will often find you in breach of your franchise agreement and will not help you to build a collaborative relationship with your franchisor.

CHAPTER EIGHT

REFLECTIVE QUESTIONS

1. Does the franchisor share the national marketing calendar with its franchisees? How often?

2. Does the franchisor have dedicated marketing team members to help franchisees with local and regional marketing efforts?

3. Does the franchisor make its marketing materials, specifically digital assets and TV and radio spots, available for franchisees wishing to amplify national programs in their local market?

4. Have you reached into the community of franchisees to learn from their previous local marketing efforts?

NOTES & REFLECTIONS

PRINCIPLE THREE

Community Connections Help Your Business Thrive

CHAPTER NINE

Why Community Relationships Matter

The one area of the franchised business model I consistently saw as an opportunity amongst the franchise community, regardless of the brand, is a need for more focus on deepening ties into the community the franchisee operates in. It cannot be overstated that strong community relationships lead to enhanced sales results and a more attractive employer value proposition, increasing your talent pools in a very competitive labor market across much of North America. Let's examine why community connections matter when building sales and how they help you with your recruiting and hiring efforts.

A recent survey conducted in the US found that an impressive 84% of people want to shop locally because they know that spending their money with the small businesses within their community goes a long way to enhancing the community for everyone [23]. Whether that's because of job creation, more significant tax contributions that support local programs, or because they know the business owners and want to help them, tapping into the tidal wave of support for small businesses in a post-COVID world is essential to success.

Growing top-line sales is always on the mind of the most successful franchisees; they constantly strive to increase and enhance their business results. Yet often, their first approach is to hit the discount line by looking for new discounted offers to get the job done. While executing strong local store marketing programs has its place, not at the expense of community engagement. It's not one or the other. Ignoring the benefits that can come from a community that rallies around your business 365 days a year and not only during periods of deep discount offers is a critical mistake.

Strong community relationships and partnerships are extremely valuable to your franchised business. Community awareness drives word-of-mouth marketing, something not to be overlooked. An interesting study by V. Kumar published in the Harvard Business Review tried to quantify how valuable word-of-mouth advertising is. He found that the referral value of a happy, loyal customer was worth more than just their lifetime spend at the business; in fact, their analysis found that the referral value was often as much as double to four times their lifetime spend [24].

Understanding that every single customer you win over to your business through strong community partnerships and support could yield up to four times the sales of that one customer is critical to making your community efforts count. To help customers who want to be advocates for your local business, you need to make it easy for them to provide feedback and testimonials to their friends and family that you can also use in your social media marketing efforts. Consider implementing a referral program instead of or alongside your loyalty program. Kumars' research suggests that most referrals come not from your most loyal customers, termed 'loyalists,' not even the second most loyal customers, called 'champions'. The most referrals came from a third group of customers called 'advocates'; they referred more new customers than any other group in the study [25].

When trying to understand how vital building loyalty within your community is to your business results, the final consideration is how you execute your business operations. None of the tactics you develop to deepen community ties will mean anything if your operations aren't making customers happy. Your efforts will be wasted, resulting in the opposite of sales-building referrals, with people in the community actively sharing their negative experiences with friends and family or, worse yet, on social media for the whole community to see. Consistent execution is critical to your success here. One cannot go without the other. So, before you start marketing your business on the outside and working to drive the community into your four walls, you must first ensure your business consistently operates to standard.

Another benefit of strong community relationships that gets even less attention from franchisees than the positive impacts those relationships can have on top-line sales is the impact those same relationships can have on their ability to hire new employees. Many franchisees understand that most of their business will come from those who work, live, and shop in their community. Yet, they fail to draw the connection that those same people could be potential employees or have children who could be potential employees. Your reputation is the driving force behind people determining if they want to work for you or refer someone they know to work for you. Additionally, your connection to and support of the local community is one of the main criteria Generation Z uses when deciding where they work. They are not a demographic to take lightly. By 2026, this generation will be the largest generational cohort, so figuring out how to attract them to your workplace is critical, and community is a vital tool to help you.

Unlike the other generations, Gen Z started out with a socially conscious perspective and didn't have to adapt to it like the other cohorts. They are incredibly passionate about how the businesses they support, either with their dollars as a customer or their time as an employee, act towards the environment, giving back and community service. Formal volunteering efforts top their list of ways to give back personally [26]. If they see you and your business doing volunteer work in the community, primarily if geared towards at-risk groups or keeping the neighborhood clean with environmental work, you'll likely earn their respect and trust, making your business somewhere they would feel proud to work.

Another big reason to ensure your business has a strong presence in the community is to capture the growing number of people who want to work close to where they live and prioritize that above all else in their job search. A recent study published in Smallbiztrends.ca found that an impressive 49% of people ranked the proximity of the business to their house as the main reason for accepting a job offer [27]. Knowing this is a preference for many and that this number will likely do nothing but grow, it's essential that you position yourself as an employer of choice in the community and actively promote why working for your business over others in the area is the way to go.

It's also worth mentioning here that in many retail and hospitality franchises, it's often young people, perhaps with their first-ever job, that work in these industries. If your business aligns with their community-focused values, you could have a loyal employee for several years, perhaps even while they finish high school and college, decreasing turnover, an often-hidden cost on your P&L, once again enhancing your unit economics. If you succeed at attracting these kids and create the right environment for them to thrive in, enjoy their work, and make meaningful social connections, you could also consider implementing another type of referral program, but this one geared towards your employees referring their friends to come and join the team. Numerous studies have shown that referrals are the single best source of hire [28] across many industries and job functions because they are more likely to fit your business's culture than those who haven't been referred to you by an existing employee.

All of this to say, don't underestimate the power of your reputation within the community to build repeat and referral business and for its ability to enhance your recruiting efforts by attracting young, community-minded local talent that, if all goes well, could lead to a steady stream of referrals, and new employee hires.

CHAPTER NINE

REFLECTIVE QUESTIONS

1. How are you currently building relationships within your community?

2. Do you have a community map listing the organizations in your local area?

3. Do you make it easy for your customers to leave feedback about your business online?

4. Do you have a program that encourages your loyal customers to refer their friends and family to your business?

5. How are you currently trying to recruit new employees from your community?

6. Do you have an employee referral program?

NOTES & REFLECTIONS

CHAPTER TEN

Building Community Relationships That Last

Now that you understand the tremendous value of strong community relationships to your business, it's time to discuss how you prioritize reaching into the community to build and sustain those relationships. After all, understanding that you need to prioritize this part of the business is different than getting out there and getting it done. In this chapter, we'll dig into three core areas of community work that will help you advance your relationships, get connected with other business owners, and last but certainly not least, I'll shed some light on some community-building programs that I've seen work to save you some trial and error. Let's jump in.

One of the easiest ways to promote yourself as a business owner who believes in and supports the local community is for you and your business to support the local community wherever and whenever possible. Walk the walk, so to speak. Trust is built over time with a series of actions matching those of the words you speak; it's no different here. It's not enough to say that the community is important to you; you must act that out in real life too. Look closely at all the products and services your business needs to operate. Can you shift any of the services you need to a local option? What about print materials? Can you shift that spend to a local printer instead of one of the big box retailers or ordering online? Reviewing your monthly invoices and service agreements can help you analyze each line of your P&L to see what opportunities there are to spend more money locally.

Another best practice to help you understand your trading area and all the businesses, community groups, schools, etc., that surround your business is to create a master community partners list. While you may be unable to support everyone around you with your business spending, think about your personal expenditures too. Where do you get your vehicle serviced? Which restaurants do you visit? Barbershops? You get the idea, if you can shop and support local, either for business or personal spending, do so. If you want the community to support you, you need to support the community. Remember, there are other ways to support community businesses that don't involve you spending money there. Consider creating a weekly 'surprise and delight' calendar, a tool to plan which community businesses you'll drop by with a few items from your menu, retail product samples, or a gift certificate for one of your services. This is a great way to either introduce yourself if you haven't been there before or as a way to say thank you for their support of your business. If you list all the companies within a 10-minute drive from you, plot them out on a calendar, and visit one or two a week, you'll be surprised at the relationships you'll forge and the business you'll drive just by 'surprising and delighting' your neighbors!

As you embark on diverting your business spending back into your community, one small word of caution is to be careful with any products your franchisor requires you to buy from a preferred vendor. Read your franchise agreement closely to understand what aspects of the supply chain are protected by the franchise agreement, and if you have questions or need more clarity, reach out to the purchasing team at your franchisor to discuss. These types of protected areas are common in the retail and hospitality industries. The scale of buying for a chain often dictates better pricing and proprietary menu items usually require adherence to a recipe for the chain to deliver on the consistency of products across the system. Of course, ensuring the vendors chosen to supply for the business are vetted for food safety precautions is paramount to the success of a restaurant brand. That said, your franchisor may also have a process in place by which you can present your local supplier as a viable option that meets the standards your franchisor has set out, and you may be able to get their approval to switch to someone local.

Another opportunity to build and advance business relationships within your community is to actively get involved with the myriad of small business associations in many parts of North America. For example, seeking out your local Chamber of Commerce is a great way to build relationships and network with your business community. The Chamber not only hosts events where you can get face time with business owners in your local area, but they often do a great job of keeping the business community informed about new policies that local or federal governments may be considering and how you can voice your concern or support for such initiatives. Due to the size and scope of its mandate to help small business owners thrive, the Chamber often offers various discounts on products and services related to running a small business. Think insurance, shipping, professional services, etc. Those preferred partnerships can be a great way to access top-rated services at more affordable rates.

The Chamber of Commerce is one partner that can help you advance your community efforts and build your business brand amongst other business owners; there are others to consider. One great example of a small business support organization that doesn't get enough fanfare is the National Federation for Independent Businesses (NFIB). The NFIB is a network of more than 300,000 business owners that collectively work together to advocate for small businesses and gain access to upcoming research trends or policy decisions that may impact them. They also offer important member benefits like access to human resource support, which can prove very valuable as small businesses often don't have the financial means to have an HR professional on staff. Yet, one of the most significant risks to a small business is the lack of employer and employee rights knowledge. Reaching out to HR professionals when you need them can save you from costly reputational and financial damage to your business. In Canada, the Canadian Federation of Small Business (CFIB) acts similarly to the NFIB and is absolutely worth the small price of an annual membership. For more on the National Federation for Independent Business, check out https://www.nfib.com/new-membership-benefits/ and the for the Canadian Federation for Independent Business, head over here https://www.cfib-fcei.ca/en/membership-benefits to learn more.

In this chapter, we've covered how to leverage both your business and personal spending to advance your support for the local business community and how joining the local Chamber of Commerce, NFIB, or the CFIB can help you access expertise, networking events, and strategic advice that you otherwise wouldn't have access to. These are excellent ways to build a reputation amongst the business community as someone who cares about supporting and advocating for a vibrant local business environment. The final piece of your community plan relates to how you spend what I call the community marketing budget. This is the pool of money you make available for things like offering a small discount to community organizations of choice, such as first responders or members of a local church or school. Or for giveaways, when community members come calling for donations they'll use as prizes to raise funds for their project or non-profit organization. All these causes are worthwhile; however, as a small business owner, you can't support everyone whenever they ask; it's just not feasible.

One of the best ways to use your community marketing funds is to design mutually beneficial programs. A great example of this is something called an earn-back program. These programs are relatively easy to set up and greatly benefit you and the community. They can be used for schools, churches, not-for-profit groups, little leagues, adult sports teams, etc. They work by having the community group rally their members to become customers at your local business. After they visit, they keep their receipts and give them to the business owner directly or to a specified community organization member, who, in turn, gives them to the business owner on a designated day each month. The business owner tallies up the receipts once or twice a year and cuts a donation cheque, based on an agreed-upon percentage, back to the church, school, sports team, etc., as an 'earn back' they can use for whatever their organization needs.

I've seen this program used with tremendous success. Schools that, through the help of the business owner, could now buy band instruments, sports equipment, or art supplies. Churches that could now afford new songbooks and bibles or host youth outings because the congregation supported the local business knowing that every dollar they spent there would result in an 'earn back' for their church. These are compelling ways to partner in the community that are mutually beneficial. So instead of offering a discount to select individuals at your business, promote these earn-back partnerships as a way to give back in meaningful and impactful ways.

CHAPTER TEN

REFLECTIVE QUESTIONS

1. Do you know which small business associations operate in your community? Are you a member of those associations?

2. How do you and your business support other local businesses in the community?

3. What other businesses, groups, and organizations surround your local business?

4. Which of those local groups or organizations may benefit from an annual 'earn back' program?

NOTES & REFLECTIONS

CHAPTER ELEVEN

Strengthening Your Online Community

The days of treating the online social media world as a secondary approach to building community relationships are long gone. The emergence of Gen Z, who will overtake the Millennials and become the largest consumer demographic by 2026 [29], have lived their entire lives online. They had tablets and smartphones in their hands before they could walk. They not only spend much of their day interacting with friends and groups online, but they've

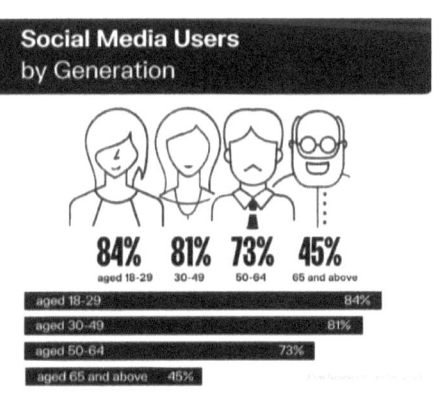

taken the online review world started by the Millennials to a whole other level. Ignoring these cohorts and failing to adapt your community-building strategies to the online world is a mistake. In this chapter, we'll cover three specific digital tactics that every franchisee needs to thrive in their online communities: building your online presence, interacting with customer feedback and reviews, and leveraging online tools that help you understand your neighborhood. Let's jump in!

Building online community relationships is now equally as important as building relationships in your actual community. Your strategy is integral to reaching younger demographics and turning them into lifelong customers.  Understanding which social media platforms will help you speak to which demographics is essential. Facebook is still the market leader regarding daily users and is an important part of your strategy. Of course, to do this, your business will need a Facebook page that should be used to engage with your customers directly. Most internet users research companies and brands online; it's especially common with Gen Z [30]. Think about how you launch new products, conduct giveaways, talk about community support programs, and promote your hiring initiatives.

Daily engagement on Facebook is a good start when considering how to build your online community; it's also a rich source of customer feedback, especially if you drive your customers to leave reviews, but we'll get to that in a moment. Another consideration often missed by franchisees in their approach to using Facebook is the group function, and it's a significant opportunity. Spend some time searching for the groups in your community, and you'll be surprised at what you find. Mothers' groups, church groups, hiking and outdoor groups, gaming groups, and so on, and so on, you get my point. Find the groups that are relevant to your business and join them. If the administrator of the group page doesn't allow business pages to join, consider joining with your personal Facebook account and interacting as the business owner. It's a great way to build your brand and relationships in online community groups relevant to your small business.

The other social media platform that has taken the Gen Z world by storm is TikTok. At the time of writing this book, the platform, while under scrutiny in the US because of data security concerns [31], is still operating. It's where you need to be if attracting younger consumers is one of your business objectives. Every day more and more companies are finding ways to use TikTok to help support their business needs. In 2020 when Chipotle needed to hire 10,000 new employees across the US, they were one of the first brands to use TikTok as a recruitment platform. They had great success with their campaign delivering an additional 7% of resumes through that channel alone [32]. So, whether you want to use TikTok to drive a younger customer demographic to your business or increase your employer brand exposure to a younger demographic, TikTok must be considered.

Another significant impact the online community has on your business is the increased importance of online reviews. Online reviews, started by the Millennials, have reached a whole new level with Gen Z. Often, this demographic will read over five online reviews of a product or service before purchasing [33]. So actively managing where your reviews are coming from and engaging with those customers promptly and meaningfully will go a very long way in how this generational cohort feels about you and your company. Remember to consider all the places your customers could leave a review of your business; it's not just social media. Platforms like Yelp, Google, and Trip Advisor also have substantial online communities that actively use these review platforms to share their customer experiences, the good and the bad.

As a franchised business owner, customer reviews can significantly impact your unit economics. As discussed in chapter five, positive reviews can drive additional customers, and top-line sales, so paying

The Impact of Positive Customer Experience

71% of consumers who have had a positive experience with a brand on social media are likely to recommend the brand to their friends and family.

(Forbes, 2018)

attention to your star rating is essential. Asking customers who have had a great experience interacting with your business to leave a review online is a great way to drive referrals and repeat customer visits. Don't be afraid to use something like a social media review card that you can hand out to customers you know you've serviced well, with links to where they can leave a review about their experience online. It's a great way to drive engagement with your online community.

Equal focus is required when dealing with any negative reviews that have been left about a customer's experience, so taking them seriously will serve you well. There are great insights that can be aggregated from negative reviews. Approach them as an opportunity to learn and evaluate how your operations are performing. You can make meaningful enhancements that will impact your customers' experience. Remember, though, when someone leaves a negative review, engage with them immediately; if more than 24 hours pass between them leaving the review and someone from your company reaching out, in the eyes of Gen Z, this is too long. Also, consider that the same way you would deal with a customer complaint in person applies online; don't be defensive. Offer to give them a call to get more feedback and take the conversation offline. Don't forget that the whole online world is reading your response when dealing with these customer complaints.

Another important aspect of building an online community is to consider the tools available to help you understand the demographics of the people and the businesses in your local trading area. You no longer need to get in your car and drive on every street with a pen and notebook, trying to figure out who your neighbors are. It's super easy these days to figure out how many people live in each neighborhood and their annual household income so that you can make more informed marketing decisions. Check out the Canada Post online marketing tools [34] and the US Postal Service tools [35] as a first step; so much rich information exists for small business owners here.

Additionally, using Google Maps to zoom in and look at all the schools, churches, community groups, businesses large and small, recreation centers, etc., is a great way to understand precisely what partnership opportunities exist around you. A best practice I've seen used by many franchisee groups is to create a master list of all the organizations that fall into the above categories and use that information to create their 'surprise and delight' calendars where each week, someone from the business visits these local groups to drop off some samples or a gift certificate for them to use in an employee draw. Starbucks is the master at using this technique; it's how they successfully entrenched themselves in communities around the world. It is a terrific way to get out of your four walls and meet the folks who work, play, or go to school close to your business. A small gift is a terrific way to open doors and help your community get to know you and your business.

CHAPTER ELEVEN

REFLECTIVE QUESTIONS

1. How does your business use social media to build an online community?

2. Are you active on Facebook, Instagram, and TikTok to connect with all demographics in your online community?

3. How are you currently leveraging online tools to gain valuable insights about those who live in your local trading area?

4. Are you using social media to build your employer brand to help you hire new employees in this challenging labour market?

5. How do you manage online reviews?

6. Do you act immediately on any trends in the feedback related to how your business operates?

NOTES & REFLECTIONS

PUTTING IT ALL TOGETHER

Operating a successful franchised business takes time and effort. It isn't enough to excel in just one or two of these principles; you must focus and deliver in all three areas. That's the secret to success. I've worked with many very successful single-unit and multi-unit franchisees over the years, and all of them put significant effort into, first and foremost, how they ran their operations, working towards consistently meeting the needs of their customers day in and day out. If you are wondering where to start on this journey, start here. Everything becomes much easier when you can confidently say that your location/locations are consistently executing the brand standards every day. It will be hard to have a strong collaborative relationship with your franchisor if you aren't delivering in this area, as upholding the brand standards is a core tenant of most franchise agreements. I would suggest that looking outside your four walls to build community relationships and implement local marketing efforts is a mistake if you aren't consistently meeting your customer's expectations. Not only will you waste precious time and resources that could be spent on enhancing your operations, but you'll suffer the double whammy of delivering a poor customer experience to new customers, driving them to a competitor instead. So double down on your operational execution first.

Once you're confident that you're delivering a consistently well-executed customer experience, it's time to start looking at how to build your employer and consumer brand in your local community. A solid effort to support your community in mutually beneficial ways and amplifying your franchisor's national marketing efforts within your local community are the best things you can do to drive top-line sales, ultimately driving sound unit economics. In a world of limited resources, focusing first on what you have immediate control over is an excellent place to start. Consistently well-executed operations and efforts to build your brand through strong community connections will almost always yield strong business results. Once these areas are firing on all cylinders, looking at your relationship with your franchisor is a good next step.

Building a collaborative, mutually beneficial relationship with your franchisor is important. Respectfully asking questions about how the employees working in the franchisor's various departments collaborate to enhance franchisee success is a fair question that the best franchisors should have no difficulty answering. It warrants a conversation if you have concerns about a specific business area. Remember, if you're doing everything you can to make your business successful, getting clarity about areas of concern you may have related to your franchisor is a worthwhile conversation to have. Use the various communication tools we discussed earlier. Whether that's your FAC member, your regional manager, or directly to the executive team, it doesn't matter as much which channel you use, just that the feedback finds its way to the right person or department. Nothing will change in the system if challenges aren't respectfully escalated, and it's very likely, especially in more extensive franchised systems, that others are experiencing the same or similar challenges. Strong collaboration between franchisees and franchisors is the unlock to fixing issues and keeping the system strong and healthy for everyone.

Whether you're a franchisee already or considering which franchise to invest in, my best advice is to review the reflective questions I've included at the end of each chapter. These questions can be used as interview questions by those currently shopping around for a franchise to invest in, as the commitment, both financially and in your time, is significant. These questions can also help existing franchisees evaluate their current franchised business success and how their franchisor is working to promote a strong and healthy system for everyone.

The franchisee-franchisor relationship is unique in that the individuals who become entrepreneurs and those who pursue a corporate career path are cut from different cloths, yet they need each other to succeed. A franchised system can only succeed and grow when franchisees invest in and operate the franchised business units. Likewise, the franchisees can only succeed by buying into a franchise with a strong team of employees who design and maintain a proven operating system and compelling marketing programs that help deliver sound unit economics with an experienced executive team at the helm. Both stakeholders are responsible for upholding their end of the agreement, and when they do, mutual success is often the result.

SOURCES

Introduction

1. Tucker, Seiler Michelle. "70 Percent of All Businesses Fail. Make Sure Yours Isn't One of The.", Inc.com, 13 May 2022, https://www.inc.com/michelle-seiler-tucker/70-percent-of-all-businesses-fail-make-sure-yours-isnt-one-of-them.html

2. Findaro, Patrick. "Franchises With the Lowest Failure Rates." Vetted Biz, 3 Mar. 2023, https://www.vettedbiz.com/100-lowest-failure-rates/

3. Daskowski, Don. "The Rise of Franchise Consultants After the Pandemic." Forbes, 23 Aug. 2021, https://www.forbes.com/sites/forbesbusinesscouncil/2021/08/25/the-rise-of-franchise-consultants-as-a-result-of-the-pandemic/?sh=77402f6b1cd2

4. 2022 Canadian Franchise Awards of Excellence, The Canadian Franchise Association. 11 Apr. 2022, https://cfa.ca/aofe-winners-2022/

5. 2022 Canadian Franchise Awards of Excellence,

The Canadian Franchise Association. 11 Apr. 2022, https://cfa.ca/aofe-winners-2022/

6. "The Ten Best Restaurant Franchises in Canada." Top Franchise, 22 Jun. 2021, https://topfranchise.com/articles/the-10-best-restaurant-franchises-in-canada/

Chapter One

7. Miller, Kelly. "10 Characteristics of Successful Entrepreneurs." Harvard University, 7 Jul. 2020, https://online.hbs.edu/blog/post/characteristics-of-successful-entrepreneurs

8. Gino, Francesca. "The Business Case for Curiosity." Harvard Business Review, Oct. 2018, https://hbr.org/2018/09/the-business-case-for-curiosity#the-business-case-for-curiosity

9. Gino, Francesca. "The Business Case for Curiosity." Harvard Business Review, Oct. 2018, https://hbr.org/2018/09/the-business-case-for-curiosity#the-business-case-for-curiosity

10. Tucker, Seiler Michelle. "70 Percent of All Businesses Fail. Make Sure Yours Isn't One of The.", Inc.com, 13 May 2022, https://www.inc.com/michelle-seiler-tucker/70-percent-of-all-businesses-fail-make-sure-yours-isnt-one-of-them.html

11. Dorie, Clark. "Google's 20% Rule Shows Exactly How Much Time You Should Spend Learning

New Skills." CNBC, 7 Jan. 2022, https://www.cnbc.com/2021/12/16/google-20-percent-rule-shows-exactly-how-much-time-you-should-spend-learning-new-skills.html

12. Trivedi, Suryakant. "The Strategy That Makes 3M an Innovation Powerhouse." The Strategy Story, 27 May 2021, https://thestrategystory.com/2021/05/27/3m-innovation-strategy/

13. Kotter, John. "The Eight Steps for Leading Change." Kotter Inc., https://www.kotterinc.com/methodology/8-steps/

14. Turning Knowing into Doing. "9 Keys to Successful Collaboration.", Discovery into Action, 28 July 2017, https://discoveryinaction.com.au/9-keys-to-successful-collaboration/

Chapter Two

15. Miles, Kerry. "Understanding Franchise Rebates." Franchise Ed, 7 Feb. 2018, https://www.franchise-ed.org.au/franchising/franchise-management/understanding-franchise-rebates/

16. Gupta, Amit. "The Failure and Success Rate of Franchises in 2022." Dr. Franchises, 13 Jan. 2023,

https://drfranchises.com/failure-success-rate-for-a-franchise/

17. Deloitte. "The 2016 Deloitte Millennial Survey." Deloitte Touche Tohmatsu Limited, 2016, https://www2.deloitte.com/content/dam/Deloitte/global/Documents/About-Deloitte/gx-millenial-survey-2016-exec-summary.pdf

Chapter Three

18. Cobban, Paul, Nair, Rahul, Painchaud, Natalie. "Breaking Down the Barriers to Innovation." Harvard Business Review, Dec. 2019, https://hbr.org/2019/11/breaking-down-the-barriers-to-innovation

Chapter Four

19. Pajaron, Tess. "Internal Communication is the Cornerstone of Good Collaboration." E27, 12 Jun. 2017, https://e27.co/internal-communication-cornerstone-good-collaboration-7-ways-organisation-can-communicate-better-20170612/

20. Clark, Larry. "Navigating Complexity, Managing Polarities." Harvard University, 17 Dec. 2018, https://www.harvardbusiness.org/navigating-complexity-managing-polarities/

Chapter Five

21. Sullivan, Laurie. "The Impact of Star Ratings and Reviews on Revenue." Media Post, 9 Aug. 2019, https://www.mediapost.com/publications/article/339083/the-impact-of-star-ratings-and-reviews-on-revenue.html

22. Wikipedia. "1992 & 1993 E.Coli Outbreak", Wikipedia, March 2023, https://en.wikipedia.org/wiki/1992%E2%80%931993_Jack_in_the_Box_E._coli_outbreak

Chapter Nine

23. ZypMedia. "Customers Want to Support Their Local Economy by Supporting Local Businesses." Cision PR Newswire, 28 May 2020, https://www.prnewswire.com/news-releases/consumers-want-to-support-their-local-economy-by-supporting-local-businesses-according-to-a-survey-by-zypmedia-301066610.html

24. Kumar, V, Peterson, Andrew, Leone, Robert P. "How Valuable is Word of Mouth." Harvard Business Review, Oct. 2007, https://hbr.org/2007/10/how-valuable-is-word-of-mouth

25. Kumar, V, Peterson, Andrew, Leone, Robert P. "How Valuable is Word of Mouth." Harvard

Business Review, Oct. 2007, https://hbr.org/2007/10/how-valuable-is-word-of-mouth

26. Fontelera, Kristy. "Gen Z Values: What You Need to Know." Non-Profit Pro, 2 Jan. 2020, https://www.nonprofitpro.com/post/gen-z-core-values-what-you-need-to-know/

27. Babu, Sandeep, "49% of Employees Say They Want to Work Close to Home." Small Business Trends, 6 Dec. 2022, https://smallbiztrends.com/2019/09/office-location.html Babu

28. Flynn, Jack. "25 Incredible Employee Referral Statistics.", Zippia the Career Experts, 27 Feb. 2023, https://www.zippia.com/advice/employee-referral-statistics/

Chapter Eleven

29. NCR. "Generation Z Characteristics: What Business Leaders Should Know About the Next Wave of Consumers." NCR Payment Solutions, 10 Nov. 2020, https://www.ncr.com/blogs/generation-z-characteristics-what-businesses-should-know-about-the-next-wave-of-consumers

30. Mohsin, Maryam. "Ten Social Media Statistics

You Need to Know in 2022.", Oberlo, 12 Sept. 2022, https://www.oberlo.com/blog/social-media-marketing-statistics#

31. Tolman, Joshua. "Why TikTok Might be Banned in the US." WLFA Play in the Moment, 12 Oct. 2022, https://www.wlfa.org/why-tiktok-might-be-banned-in-the-united-states/

32. Adeolu, Moyo. "Chipotle Recruits Workers with New TikTok Resume Program." Ad Age, 9 July 2021, https://adage.com/article/marketing-news-strategy/chipotle-recruits-workers-tiktoks-new-resume-program/2349481

33. Unidays. "All the Gen Z Statistics You Could Ever Ask For Right at Your Finger Tips.", Unidays, 1 Feb. 2020, https://www.genzinsights.com/hundreds-of-useful-gen-z-stats-right-at-your-fingertips

34. Business Marketing, Data Analytics, Canada Post https://www.canadapost-postescanada.ca/cpc/en/business/marketing/audience/license-data.page

35. Zip Code Data Base, US Postal Service, https://www.unitedstateszipcodes.org/zip-code-database/

www.ingramcontent.com/pod-product-compliance
Lightning Source LLC
Chambersburg PA
CBHW031920240526
45464CB00021B/608